CONNECT THE DOTS

A PLAYBOOK TO HELP YOU CONNECT TO YOUR CUSTOMERS AND PROFITS

JOHN LINCOLN

AuthorHouse™
1663 Liberty Drive
Bloomington, IN 47403
www.authorhouse.com
Phone: 1-800-839-8640

Published by AuthorHouse 10/29/2012

ISBN: 978-1-4772-8616-6 (sc)
ISBN: 978-1-4772-8614-2 (hc)
ISBN: 978-1-4772-8612-8 (e)

Library of Congress Control Number: 2012920689

DEDICATION

To my darling Carol and all my children,
whom I love with all my heart and soul.

I owe everything that I am, to them.

FOREWORD

John Lincoln has been a member of my larger du team since September 2008. I have observed with pride as he has driven du's growth in the B2B segment. John is an excellent people manager who is able to appreciate his team, see the big picture and take the risks necessary to establish our B2B market share in this vibrant market.

We are proud that one of our fellow 'du-ers' has published his first book, *Connect the Dots*. This is an up-to-date, practical, informative business guide and playbook that will be useful for every entrepreneur. I recommend small and medium business owners and would-be entrepreneurs read this with attention, as it will help them avoid many pitfalls.

I wish John continued success in his career and as a writer.

Osman Sultan

CEO, du
Dubai

September 2012

FOREWORD

I have known John Lincoln since 1997 when we both were seconded to Japan in J Phone and from 2002 to 2004, when John was a member of my larger team in Japan Telecom.

I found John to be strategic thinker who is highly results-focused. John's adaptive nature and capabilities has made him an excellent people manager who was able to mentor and motivate across cultures and language barriers. I always noticed that John saw the big picture and was able to strategize quickly and convincingly – and take the big leap of faith whenever needed.

And now, he has written a book! *Connect the Dots* is an excellent read, full of information, practical advice and lessons that could only come from experience. I love its tone and am certain it will be an invaluable playbook for men and women who are ready to brave the entrepreneurial waters.

Well done John!

Bill Morrow

CEO, Vodafone Hutchison Australia
Sydney

Former Chief Executive Officer at Pacific Gas a
nd Electric Company, San Francisco, US

Former CEO, Vodafone Europe, Vodafone Japan,
Vodafone UK and Japan Telecom

September 2012

ABOUT THE AUTHOR

With more than 30 years of senior level management experience in start-ups, telecom giants and technology companies across the globe, John Lincoln has experienced success and failures from boom to bust.

Currently, he is the Vice President – Enterprise Marketing for du in the UAE and has representative responsibility to deliver the B2B (enterprise, large corporate and SMEs) revenue and profitability for this telecommunications company that has changed the face of public telecommunications in one of the world's fastest growing regions.

John has witnessed the early days of telecommunications when a few kb/sec was deemed as high speed access. John foresaw the huge potential of the telecommunications industry as early as the 1990s, and then decided to pursue a Master of Science degree in Telecommunications from Golden Gate University, San Francisco, after completing his MBA from the same institution.

John has a truly global perspective. A transplanted American, he has worked in countries such as Japan, India, the UK, Malaysia, Thailand and Brazil, apart from the US. He has held senior management positions in global companies such as Vodafone, Japan Telecom, Bharti Airtel and AT & T and has had the privilege of hiring and managing large multicultural teams and working in different and very challenging market conditions.

Through it all, John has grown and learnt from his – and other people's – successes and failures. He started and ran small businesses, risking a lot of his capital and working round-the-clock. But the businesses failed, because he "didn't know what he knows now". That led to him resuming his corporate career which he continues to cherish.

A keen and widely read blogger (http://www.johnlincoln.biz), John turns his work and life experiences into easy-to-read and easy-to-adapt essays and guidelines. He is also a regular contributor to the SME Advisor Middle East, Kippreport and Intelligent SME, three publications read widely by the multicultural business community in the region.

John lives between beautiful San Francisco (where his family resides) and never-sleeping Dubai and travels across the world. He once used to fly single engine planes for fun, but now settles for voracious reading of business books, attempting to bridge the culture gap at a personal level and getting up to date with the latest technology and business ideas. An avid observer of good business practices, John continues to advise small and medium enterprises on what drives innovation, entrepreneurship, sustainability and growth.

INTRODUCTION

Let me tell you a real life story. A close friend invested all his hard-earned savings into establishing a motel business in the west coast of the United States. He made sure it was in a brilliant location and offered a compelling proposition to his potential customers. Then he set about hiring the all-important general manager. He came back to me after a month and said, "John, I have found a great guy. But I can't hire him." "Why ever not?" I asked. "Because we are so different as people!" my friend said. I could only stop and stare…

My friend failed to see how the effectiveness and competency of the man mattered more than his provenance. He more than spectacularly failed to connect the dots between his customers and the bottom line.

He is not alone.

I have seen many great ideas fail, particularly SMEs, because the owners/managers have failed to connect the vital dots. As children, we learn to see the big picture – and take the first key step at self-expression – by connecting the dots. As adult entrepreneurs, this is exactly what we need to learn all over again. All the time.

With more than 30 years of global experience ranging from working in start-ups and technology companies to telecom giants, I have been fortunate to work in countries as far apart as the US, Japan, UK, India, the UAE and others. I have high-fived through the bubble and held many hands during the recession.

Through it all, I have been deeply awed by the drive, zeal and entrepreneurship of small businesses. I have been strongly inspired by how they commit capital and take tremendous risks day in and day out. Through their dedication and commitment, small and medium businesses drive the larger economies of their countries.

Then again, I have been acutely distressed by how many SMEs are opportunistic rather than strategic in nature. Most small business owners do not have the resources that large companies take for granted. They don't have the money to spend on expensive management consultants and training programs. They do not think of growth and sustainability, but only work on generating quick profits.

As a result, employees are often miserable and businesses fail daily. A drastic consequence that can be corrected if entrepreneurs take a minute to sit back, think and PLAN.

Connect the Dots is my attempt to create a playbook for the entrepreneur, a take-everywhere-you-go guide to surviving – and flourishing – in business. Whether you are young or old, woman or man, about to start off on your own or merely thinking of doing so one day, this book will help you see your path clearly.

We all know about virtuous and vicious cycles. In this book, I help you to identify the simple steps that will accentuate the virtuous and disrupt the vicious cycle. Know your exit strategy before you start your business; entice and tempt your customers to sin; the eight-steps of great sales leadership; smarter business management; how to engage in a price war as all war is deception... these are just some of the chapters you will find discussed in *Connect the Dots.*

You will not get dry theory here. You will find a book written out of experience lived across the world. I am a transplanted American with a multi-ethnic family and I live and work in the cultural melting pots of San Francisco and Dubai. Through my work and my travels, I have been lucky to see the world as a whole.

This book, my tribute to successful small and medium businesses, is deliberately and carefully written for a cross-geography, multicultural, multiracial and multi sector audience.

Ironically, that has also been my biggest challenge: how NOT to generalize. In fact, I have a written at length on the fallacies of average! On a personal note, I have also been challenged by the dreariness of long hours of writing and have been frequently afflicted by the dreaded writer's block.

But I have persevered, through cool San Francisco nights and hot Dubai days, to think and write and plan. Think for the entrepreneur in all of us. Write for the SME owner. Plan for the businessperson afraid to take a risk.

This book is for you. Urging you to connect the dots between your business, customers and the bottom line and staying with you while you draw that line with a firm hand. Do let me know how it goes at johnlincoln@outlook.com

Happy entrepreneuring!

John Lincoln
Author, Dubai and San Francisco
September 2012

CONTENTS

SECTION 1:
GETTING STARTED OUT ON THE RIGHT TRACK

SECTION 2:
PUTTING TOGETHER THE BUSINESS PROPOSITION

SECTION 3:
GO-TO-MARKET STRATEGIES

SECTION 4:
KEY CONSIDERATIONS FOR MANAGING AND OPERATING YOUR BUSINESS

SECTION 5:
MANAGEMENT STRATEGIES TO GROW YOUR BUSINESS

SECTION

GETTING STARTED OUT ON THE RIGHT TRACK

IT'S VITAL TO **PULL YOUR COMPANY ALONG** A PATH WHICH HAS IT GENERATING STRONG CASH FLOW, AND DEMONSTRATING YEAR-ON-YEAR GROWTH.

1

KNOW YOUR EXIT BEFORE YOU TAKE THE BULL BY THE HORNS

The strategy of successful start-up (and exit)

As a business owner or investor, you will have started out with your business for any number of reasons. These could range from a need to follow your dreams, to seek financial or career independence, to pursue your hobby or passion in life, or to fulfill an ambition to make it into the big league of the business titans – the ones who adorn the covers of well-known business magazines!

Amid all the stress and excitement of getting a business up and running, one of the last things on your mind will be an exit strategy. In fact, the very notion of an exit, just as you are taking the 'bull by the horns', may seem utterly counterproductive. Who in their right mind would be contemplating an exit, when they have hardly got going?

Needless to say, there are some very good reasons for every business owner or investor to consider their exit strategy – it needs be done at the very earliest of stages, and even before the company opens its door for business! Before we consider the various exit strategies, just why is an exit strategy one of the most important factors to plan for, when there are seemingly many more important issues to tackle when starting and running a start-up?

Seven reasons why you must have an exit plan ready

There are many reasons, beyond any wished-for windfall, why an exit strategy is needed – life is full of twists and turns, some of which are avoidable and some inevitable and in every case, the timing is anything but predictable.

Divorce Most business relationships do not end on a positive note, so there is a need for a plan and a view as to why, when and how you will exit – if and when there is an irreconcilable breakdown between you and your business partners. You should plan for this to be a virtual certainty, as most relationships evolve over a period of time and you and your partners will be influenced by a myriad of people and business factors, and people and relationships change accordingly.

Death Other than the certainty of paying taxes (in most countries!), death is a certainty that needs to be planned for, beyond the obvious critical-man life insurance policies that need be put in place by the business. A concrete plan is called for, which includes a view on how dependent the business is on each of the partners, how their families will survive, and how the remaining partners will be able to conduct the business.

Disability What happens if you or a fellow director is disabled through an accident or due to ill health? Who is going to take care of them, their family, their investments and the business?

Departure When and how do you want to exit the business? How are you going to recoup your investment and tenure in a business that you have started and nurtured, for a period of time? What are your plans to ride into the sunset?

Detour How would you exit your business, if and when a new investment or business opportunity comes your way?

Deceit How would you exit your business if you found out a key stakeholder like a partner, was colluding with a customer or supplier or was being deceitful or defaulting on dues to you?

Decline in growth What are your plans if/when business growth stalls? Do you just wait, bide your time and exit gracefully, forgoing all your hard work, risk and money invested in your business?

Why planning for an exit is important for every start-up

Having established the need for an exit strategy, we should tick off a few essentials that need be taken care of when planning that exit strategy. Most entrepreneurs ignore these to their own detriment. It's unclear if they see them as an unnecessary expense or a waste of time, but if things go wrong or absurdly right, then it is this very set of actions that is going to cover you:

1 **Have rigorous,** fool-proof financial accounting methods, policies and procedures in place, from day one.

2 **Have a shareholders' agreement** that clearly spells out the rights of each founding partner.

3 **Create a tiered (preferred) class of shares** that enable you to pay out higher dividends and share of profits, and one which will ensure that you have higher voting rights.

4 **Get power of attorney documents signed** by all partners giving you the right to run your business (legally), without undue interference or limitations by other partners.

5 **In the case of a limited company with a board of directors**, get blank board resolution documents signed by all board members.

6 **Get an appointment letter attested to and signed** by all partners clearly stipulating your role as the 'Chief Executive Officer' of the company, your salary and tenure.

So what are some of the likely exit strategies?

While these suggestions seem over cautious, when an opportunity arises for an exit, or when something goes wrong with the business partnership, everyone will really appreciate that you went through the arduous task of getting the accounting and legal due diligence work done. When things go so well or so bad, inevitably cracks will appear in any partnership. The legal protection wrapped around you will pay off big time!

INITIAL PUBLIC OFFERING (IPO)

IPOs are a rarity nowadays. Of the millions of businesses in the world, only perhaps one in a thousand ever makes it to an IPO. Unless the business has the backing of well-known and solid venture funds with a track record of taking companies public, this is not an option that will touch many start-ups or small businesses.

The process of getting prepared for an IPO is expensive and cumbersome. It involves lawyers, auditors, investment bankers and consultants who are all out for their fair share of meat. During an IPO process the business and its executives are under the spotlight and subject to various regulatory compliance obligations and audits that you probably never knew existed!

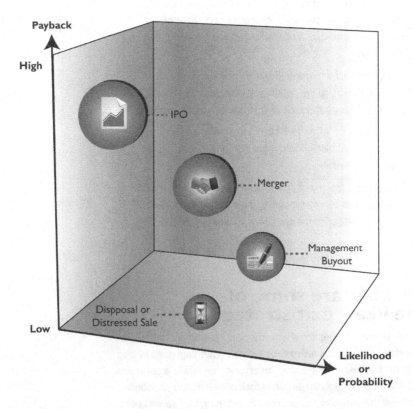

Figure I: The appeal of an exit strategy will depend on the market conditions, the business scenario and the desired outcome, with the relative payback shaped by the timing and type of the deal.

You start off the process by being the ultimate salesman, convincing investors during road shows with investment bankers that your business is worth much more than it is. By the time the business becomes a candidate for an IPO, your equity will have been well diluted, after the 'vulture' funds had agreed to invest in you and your business!

Although IPOs are glamorous and populist of exit strategies, they should not be the first option. Most entrepreneurs are still enamoured by the dot.com bubble at the beginning of this century, but don't be fooled by these and other IPO stories! That said, for a business which has a unique technology that is well protected by patents, and is funded by well known venture funds, there truly is potential to win the lottery aka IPO!

MERGER OR ACQUISITION

Getting another entity to acquire your company is one of the most common ways to exit from a business. The principle is simple – find another business that is ready, willing and able to buy your business, sell it and keep the money and occasionally get paid an earn-out or bonus of some kind, for remaining with the business and helping the new owners run the business that you have started.

Most successful small businesses are acquired by much larger public companies. What this can mean in essence is that you are in a better position than the buyer is. This is so because the folks negotiating and making the acquisition decisions are not vested on their own money but are investing other people's money. So whereas you will be negotiating a value for all your blood, sweat and tears they are often just 'employees' with little to lose.

The recommendation is to get to know as much as possible in advance about the potential acquirer. Then craft the proposition in a manner which suits the potential acquiring company, and is designed to be complimentary to its existing business portfolio. The trick is not to limit the exit to one or two suitors. Have an array of suitors and evolve your propositions over a period of time. This way, you have the potential of ratcheting a bidding war among multiple suitors, or at the very least to create a high level of perceived strategic value to a single acquirer.

DISPOSAL, DIVESTMENT OR BUY-OUT TO EMPLOYEES, FAMILY OR FRIENDS If you are a true believer (in your business) and if you are emotionally connected to your business, then selling it to a friendly buyer might be the best option. A friendly buyer could include your family, friends and/or employees who are prepared to invest their own or borrow money for a management buy-out.

Businesses that take this path will not necessarily be doing this for an outrageous monetary exit, but rather to ensure that the quality, integrity and continuity of the business is assured.

BLEED TO DEATH There are a few business owners who bleed their company dry almost on a daily basis and pay themselves a chunk of salary and bonus, irrespective of their company's performance. Some of them give themselves five to ten times the dividends that other shareholders receive. Although these activities are illegal in public companies, they are perfectly legal in private companies.

Cash is king in such companies, and the owners do not reinvest it in their business nor do they consider growing their business. They keep investments down to a minimum and withdraw cash to live off the income of these businesses.

For most businesses, cash that is taken out for personal use is no longer available to the business for reinvesting. Where the business plan deems that the company must invest to grow, then of course, this is not a viable option. There are other ways that a 'cash is king' exit could work. You could get your family to loan the business money and pay a high level of interest for the loan. This way the cash is kept in the family, safe from the taxman and away from any creditors and your preferred shareholders.

No matter what exit strategy is preferred or chosen, it is important to note that the valuation of your company is primarily driven by two factors:

- The cash flow derived from the revenue that the business generates.
- The growth that is being demonstrated year on year.

In this context it is vital to time and pace any exit to a period when cash flow is maximized (therefore your revenue) and when growth is poised to peak. This is a truism that is applicable in any professional career or business: always exit on a high note! Look around: great business leaders remain great because they exited at the peak of their company's growth!

NOTES

CASH IS THE MOST
IMPORTANT ASSET OF
ANY BUSINESS, WHATEVER
ITS SIZE – AND IS USED FOR
SHORT-TERM OPERATIONS,
PURCHASES AND
ACQUISITIONS.

PLAN! PLAN! PLAN BEFORE YOU SEEK ANY FUNDING

Planning, funding and managing cash flow

In business as in personal life, cash is the lifeline for everything we do. Managing cash flow can be a major challenge, and stands as a critical success factor for every business. Even before opening for business, one of the chief criteria a lender or investor will most closely scrutinise is your ability to generate and manage cash.

So it is important to understand some of the fundamentals that any funder, lender or investor will consider before dishing out their hard earned money to you.

If you are in the business of business, and if you need to raise funds, then the advice must be that a business plan is an imperative which calls for time, effort and money. If it is to hit all the right notes, then make sure that your business plan is **SMART**:

- Specific
- Measurable
- Actionable,
- Resourced
- Time bound

> It is not the strongest of the species that survive, not the most intelligent, but the one most responsive to change."
>
> *Charles Darwin, scientist*

First and foremost, they will examine the quality and robustness of your business plan. So get a friend to help finesse it, or better still pay a professional to write one for you: it is a vital first step that needs to be taken if you are to start out on the right footing with a new venture. A good plan will not only provide investors with the level of confidence they are seeking, it will give you the direction you will need and will help shape good decisions. The business plan needs to be organic, rather than a forgotten piece of shelfware. It is something that will need to be regularly shared and presented, reviewed and revised with your potential investors and business associates.

You cannot be all things to all people indefinitely so it is vital that the business plan is focused and time bound. If it is not, in all likelihood, is not a realistic plan! Remember these words of wisdom on business planning:

Without a plan, you cannot raise funds, let alone act or respond to changes in the whitewater environment of business. Therefore, plan! plan! plan!

Our goals can only be reached through a vehicle of a plan, in which we must fervently believe, and upon which we must vigorously act. There is no other route to success." *Unknown*

1. **Feasibility** – A business plan helps determine if your new business idea is feasible and that the business is viable and sustainable.

2. **Resources requirements** – A business plan helps identify the level of short, medium and long-term financial and human resources that are needed to commit to the venture.

3. **Risks** – A business plan helps identify all the risks in the proposed venture, as well as helping mitigate against those potential risks.

4. **Stakeholder management** – A business plan is one of the most important tools to communicate clearly to investors, lenders, business associates, employees and suppliers.

5. **Funding requirements** – A business plan is critical in identifying funding requirements and the timelines those funds are required.

6. **Commercial model** – A business plan will help establish if the commercial model and pricing of the proposition are realistic, or if some of the original assumptions should be tweaked or revised.

7. **Operating model** – A business plan will force the development of an end-to-end view of the new venture's operating model and forces everyone to map the end-to-end processes that need to be executed.

8. **Marketing plan** – A business plan is a precursor to a marketing plan.

9. **Competitors** – A business plan forces the development of market awareness and an understanding of the potential competitors, an analysis of the potential strengths and opportunities, as well as the potential weaknesses and threats to your business.

10. **People** – A business plan helps identify any skill gaps that need to be filled.

Figure 2: Ten reasons why a business plan is imperative before starting.

The twenty questions of business funding

Key factors that lenders and investors will consider before backing a business

1 **Owner credibility** – Do you have references to attest to your character and professional and/or entrepreneurial capabilities? People invest in people first!

2 **Business plan** – Do you have a well documented business plan?

3 **Vision and mission** – Do you have a clearly articulated vision and mission statement of the venture?

4 **Is the idea marketable?** – Do you have a business plan with a marketable idea? Is your market reachable? Can your proposition be marketed?

5 **Target market** – Do you have a clear view as to who your target market would be and whether the market potential is realistic or unrealistic, too narrow or has high potential for growth?

6 **Commercial model** – Do you have an absolute understanding of cash flow and how money is flowing to your business? Is it easy to explain or is it as complex as Enron? Will the other players in the industry value chain tolerate your existence and let you 'eat their lunch'?

7 **Operating model** – Do you have a well articulated process as to how your business would be run? This includes the processes on hiring, accounting, product development, sales and marketing, supply chain management and all the other processes that are required to operate your business.

8 **Business strategy** – Do you have a business strategy to execute on the plan? Is the strategy realistic?

9 **Risk mitigation** – Do you have a clear view of the potential market, technological, legal and human capital risks for your new venture? If risks have been identified, do you have a view and a plan as to how you will mitigate these risks?

10 **Profit potential** – Do you have a business plan that reflects realistic profit potential in a reasonable period of time? The annual rate of returns should be high enough to compensate the risk that a potential investor is making.

11 **Unique value proposition** – Do you know how to differentiate the business proposition in the market vis-a-vis your competitors? Are you a 'me

too' player? If you are a 'me too', you do not have much of a chance to get funding from established sources. You have to clearly articulate as to how and why you will have an edge over your competition. What are the entry barriers for others to replicate your business model? What is the window of opportunity to get scale before other imitators follow your model?

12 **Go to market model** – Do you have a clear view as how you will take your proposition to market? Do you have a view on how you will promote the business? What channels would you engage to take the product to market? How would you compensate them?

13 **Sales and marketing capability** – Do you have the right folks to market and sell your proposition? This is one of the most important functions critical for the success of your business. Having a bunch of talented technology folks alone is not going to cut it for you. Likewise, having all the marketing and sales superstars, without the relevant technology talents, is not a viable proposition.

14 **Technology** – Is the technology unique? Is it patentable? Do you have the right folks to develop the proposition? Is it easily copied or imitated?

15 **Supplier and partner commitments** – Have you secured commitment to supply from your vendors and suppliers? Are your vendors and partners reliable and dependable?

16 **Execution capability** – Are you able to execute and deliver a superb quality proposition with a high degree of probability? What are the weak points in your execution? How are you going to mitigate this weak area?

17 **Management capability** – Do you have an experienced team running the business? Are they credible? Are their experiences verifiable? Do they have the relevant functional and managerial expertise? Have they worked in the industry before? (Or, do you have your brother-in-law as your Chief Marketing Officer just because you had to hire him?)

18 **Level of risk of the owner/s** – Do you have 'skin in the game'? What have you risked for this venture? Are you counting on a full 'OPM' (Other People's Money) funding strategy?

19 **Socio-economic benefits and ethics** – Is your business legal? Is it an ethical business that investors can be proud of being associated with?

20 **Multi-scenario financial projections** – Do you have an optimistic, base case and pessimistic scenarios based financial projections for your business plan? Have you projected your income, balance sheet, and cash flow statements? Do you know well, your sources of funding (both equity and debt)? Do you know when a new injection of funding is required and how you plan to secure it?

NOTES

HAVE AN ELEVATOR PITCH: *A SUMMARIZED DESCRIPTION OF YOUR BUSINESS TO BE ARTICULATED TO POTENTIAL FUNDERS IN NO MORE THAN THREE MINUTES.*

TRADITIONAL AND ALTERNATE SOURCES OF FUNDING FOR YOUR SMALL BUSINESS

The essentials of business funding; its many sources and how to pick the right one for you

We all rely on bank loans, credit cards and personal loans from friends and family to get us through life, and it can be much the same in business – with sources like venture funds and angel investors offering other possible routes for funding.

Whatever the source in these trying economic times, traditional lending sources like banks and venture finances have raised the bar to lending, and are now very particular about who they would lend to. Therefore, it is essential for the small business owner to know what criteria the finance houses use to determine whether they will sponsor a start-up or fund the expansion of an existing business.

12 ESSENTIALS OF BUSINESS FUNDING

1 **BUSINESS PLAN** Have a coherent and robust business plan!

2 **CREDIBILITY** Establish personal credibility and reputation in your community or social circle.

3 **CREDIT** Maintain a good credit rating.

4 **CONFIDENCE** Be confident.

5 **PERSEVERANCE** Be prepared for rejections. Don't give up.

6 **PASSION** Show a sense of passion. After all, you are the Chief Believer!

7 **PITCH** Have an elevator pitch: a summarized description of your business to be articulated to potential funders in no more than three minutes.

8 **PROFESSIONAL** Dress appropriately for the business that you are in.

9 **PUNCTUAL** Always be punctual for any meetings with potential funders.

10 **PREPAREDNESS** Rehearse your business plan presentation.

11 **PRESENTATION** Have a professional looking and polished presentation summary of your business plan, as well as a detailed version of your business plan to hand with figures and forecasts that are conservative and achievable.

12 **PERSONAL** You should personally articulate your vision, mission and commercial model. It is alright to have the consultants beside you, but you should make the critical part of the pitch yourself.

Exploring the funding sources available to a start-up or expanding business

There are many funding sources available and some of them are obvious, others less so.

PERSONAL SAVINGS

Funding a business with your personal savings is not the most prudent thing to do. As most start-ups fail, it is neither smart nor sensible to put all your 'eggs in one basket'. However, if you can afford it, then using a portion of your personal savings is definitely a boost in your overall funding endevor, as it will show commitment. Potential lenders and investors like to see that their clients have some 'skin in the game', and so stand to win big with the success of their business.

Keep in mind that the journey is going to be very tough, and therefore any personal investment from you should best be sourced from the sale of an asset that you are not currently using – like an extra property or vehicle. If you do have a chunk of your own extra money sitting in a bank, by all means invest in your business of choice.

(A point to note is that, if you do have a chunk of money sitting idle in the bank, then you probably would not be reading an article on sources of funding!) A word of caution: Before investing your hard earned personal savings, take a step back and consider seriously the impact it will have on your family and yourself. If you still feel that you must, then you are probably on to something that is worth the effort and the risk.

FAMILY AND FRIENDS

Most start-ups get started with money from their immediate family or friends (this type of funding is commonly known as FFF for friends and family – and fools). If your boot-strapped company is in dire need of cash, and if you have a family member or friend willing to invest, it is a path that you should consider.

Unless you are in a bubble economy or have some unique technology patent, most friends and family are not investing in the business, but rather they are investing in you personally. A word of caution – the $10,000 that Cousin Tom dished out might come at a high price – like requests for employment for all kith and kin and/or unnecessary interference in your time and business!

Since most family and friends are investing in a person rather than a business, it is recommended that funding from friends and relatives be started off as a loan rather than an equity participation in the business. This loan should, of course, be structured with a formal agreement and repayment plan. This way, you can mitigate future unwarranted interference in your business.

SINCE MOST FAMILY AND FRIENDS ARE INVESTING IN A PERSON RATHER THAN A BUSINESS, it is recommended that funding from friends and relatives be started off as a loan rather than an equity participation in the business. This loan should, of course, be structured with a formal agreement and repayment plan. This way, you can mitigate future unwarranted interference in your business.

CREDIT CARDS

Funding a start-up or an on-going business with personal credit cards is more common than you think. About 30 years ago, it was considered "non-passé" or "not credit worthy" or imprudent to use a credit card to fund your business. Today, it is neither frowned upon nor considered risky.

Before you start on a credit card splurge for your business, be aware of the high interest rates that credit cards charge. Also do keep in mind that cash advances on a credit card carries with it much higher interest rates. Credit cards should only be used to fund emergencies in your business. Do not use credit cards to fully fund and manage your business. Credit cards should only be used as a mezzanine or stop gap measure for interim working capital or inventory management.

If you do use credit cards to fund your business, ensure that the pricing of your goods and services reflect the relatively higher interest rates that you are paying to fund your business, through the usage of credit cards. Also, ensure that you choose the credit cards from providers offering interest-free financing, for longer periods of time.

A WORD OF CAUTION Do not max out your credit card limits by paying the minimum monthly payments. If you are prone to paying the minimum payment, then this important source of funding will just not be there when you need it most! It is also one of the most expensive forms of borrowing.

ANGEL INVESTORS

The term "angel investors" originated from Broadway where wealthy folks who funded theatrical productions were called "angels". Today angel investors are generally a group of successful folks who have extra money at hand to invest. Angel investors understand the risks of start-up businesses, and therefore expect a much higher return for the increased risks that they are taking. As most start-ups fail, the increased returns that they expect are fair because it is more likely than not for them to lose a good number of their investments completely.

Before you approach a group of angel investors, it is important for you to know the objective of the angel investor. Of course, most of them are taking part in this high stakes game for the expected high returns. But do keep in mind that since most of them are successful entrepreneurs or former business executives themselves, there are other reasons why they fund start-ups. These can range from their need to keep informed of the latest trends in technology, to networking, to opening an avenue to share their business experience and networks. Therefore it is important that you position your company and yourself to match the angel investor's objectives.

Angel investors appreciate there will be a need for additional funds to scale your business. Therefore, one thing to keep in mind when you negotiate the term sheet is that you should alert the angel investor of your anticipated future funding needs. You should offer the angel investor the option to invest in subsequent rounds, as well as alert them of the high potential for dilution of their equity.

AN IMPORTANT NOTE ON ANGEL INVESTORS: If you have found an angel investor interested in your start-up and one who does not want to invest his or her money due to other commitments – an option is to leverage the angel investor's asset base and reputation to guarantee a bank loan for your business.

BANK TERM LOANS

There are many forms of bank loans available for the small business and these include everything from bank overdrafts to term loans. A bank overdraft is seldom given to start-ups with no established cash flows, however. Instead, term loans are the most common types of loans. They are very simple in that the lender provides a specific amount of money, usually at a fixed rate of interest, and there is a schedule for repaying the loan (usually in monthly or quarterly payments) over a certain amount of time.

The big question that a bank wants answered is whether you have the necessary collateral. In these trying times, an unsecured loan is a rarity and is only offered to folks or businesses with an exceptional credit history.

There is big caveat on bank loans that you should be aware – most banks will seek full recourse to the individual owner or shareholders for full recovery of the loan just in case things don't turn out the way you expected it. It is imperative, therefore, that you ensure that the business risks are mitigated before committing to a bank loan, as the consequences of a failure will affect you personally.

The requirements for a term loan are arduous and time consuming. Banks normally require a significant amount of information before they approve the loan. These can range from:

- Your detailed business plan.
- A personal guarantee for short-term loans if the collateral is insufficient.
- Your credit report.
- The type of collateral you can provide.
- Company incorporation or trading licenses.
- Your personal and financial commitment to the business.
- Financial statements of the business, for at least three years.
- Tax returns (if and where applicable), for the past three years.

TERM LOANS HAVE BOTH BENEFITS AND DRAWBACKS – they bring an ability to leverage the term loan to preserve working capital but you need to watch out for those exorbitant fees!

VENTURE CAPITAL (VC)

Funding from venture capital companies (VCs) provides medium-term committed share capital to help companies grow and succeed. The funding objectives from VCs are very different from funding sourced through bank loans. Banks charge interest for their loans and seek repayment of the capital, irrespective of whether the business succeeds or fails. VCs invest funds in exchange for an equity stake in your business and expect significant returns when they exit the business, taking a start-up to an IPO stage or selling it or their share to other equity owners.

VCs invest in businesses that have unique intellectual property or in businesses that have a unique and sustainable commercial model. VCs also generally invest in companies which are managed by experienced and capable teams that have the requisite experience to take the business to the next level.

LEASING

Many small businesses do not use leasing as a way to fund a portion of their capital requirement, yet most equipment leases rarely require down payments. If a business has or needs vehicles, machinery or equipment that needs to be purchased, leasing is an option that should seriously be considered as a way of preserving capital.

For many start-ups, the reality is that leasing may be your only real option for acquiring needed business assets. An advantage that is often overlooked is that leasing may improve certain financial indicators, such as your debt-to-equity and earnings-to-fixed-assets ratios. This is so because you are able to exclude your leased assets and their corresponding monthly rental obligations from the balance sheet, and yet are able to include the revenue derived from the assets in the income statement.

FACTORING

Factoring is useful for companies suffering a cash-flow squeeze and/or facing slow payment cycles from their customers. Small businesses can sell their invoices or accounts receivable to funding companies called factors. The factor advances most of the invoiced amount ranging from 75% to 95%, after verifying the credit worthiness of each of the small business' customers. The factor charges a factoring fee and remits the balance back to the small business. The factoring firm handles the collections allowing the company to focus on running the business rather than chasing invoices and cash collection.

Once the credit worthiness of a small business customer is

established, a small business is usually able to get the funds for invoices within 24 to 48 hours rather than waiting the usual 30 to 90 days for the customer to pay.

Traditional lenders normally look at the business creditworthiness when evaluating a loan application, whilst factors evaluate mainly the financial standing of the small business's customers. This is a tremendous boost for a small business's funding endevors, as they are able to fund their working capital through factors, even if they have little or no credit history.

ONE IMPORTANT POINT TO NOTE ABOUT FACTORING IS THAT IT CAN BE COSTLY by several basis points above a traditional lender. One other important consideration is that it will not be economical for a small business that sends out thousands of small value invoices, as the service fees that a factor charges might depend on the number of invoices issued.

GOODS OR SERVICE SALES – THE SOURCE OF ALL FUNDING

Business owners and managers have many options when it comes to funding their working capital or long-term funding requirements. The key issue to note is that the funding expense varies vastly and that the resultant costs should be baked into the pricing of your goods or services.

Do not feel dejected when funding applications are turned down. As a small business owner and risk taker, you are already special. Don't let some high and mighty bureaucrat in some large corporation tell you that you stand no chance! For inspiration, remember what Dale Carnegie said: "Most of the important things in the world have been accomplished by people who have kept on trying when there seemed to be no help at all."

NOTES

A BUSINESS CAN HAVE PLENTIFUL ASSETS ON ITS BALANCE SHEET AND GOOD PROFITABILITY, BUT IF IT IS SHORT OF LIQUIDITY BECAUSE ITS ASSETS CANNOT READILY BE CONVERTED INTO CASH THEN IT WILL QUICKLY RUN INTO PROBLEMS.

MANAGING THE LIFELINE OF YOUR BUSINESS – CASH FLOW AND WORKING CAPITAL MANAGEMENT

What the terms actually mean and how to keep the lifeblood of your business flowing energetically

It is vitally important that business owners and managers fully grasp the concept of cash flow management and understand that the timing of cash flows can determine whether a business will thrive or perish. There are various strategies and tactics that come into play to successfully manage cash flow, or working capital management as it is also commonly known, and these need to be deployed every single business day.

So let's first look at what makes up working capital, how it is best managed and why it is so critical to business success...

Understanding working capital management: money today to make money tomorrow!

Working capital is the sum of all the items on the balance sheet that includes cash, short-term debt, investments, inventory, debtors (receivables), payables (creditors) and so forth. So the management of working capital involves managing inventories, accounts receivable and payable, and cash to maintain adequate levels of net working capital – the difference between all the current assets of the business and its current liabilities.

Current Assets	Current Liabilities
Inventory	
Sundry debtors (account receivables)	Sundry creditors (account payables)
Cash and bank balances	Provisions
Loans and advances	Short-term loans

Keep in mind that current assets have a short life span and that they should be quickly transformed into other asset forms. For example, cash is used to acquire raw materials or supplies and these supplies or materials are converted into a finished product, service or marketed proposition. Those that are sold on credit are converted into account receivables and finally into cash when the payment for them is received.

The everyday control of working capital is often referred to as cash flow management, cash management and/or liquidity management.

A business can have plentiful assets on its balance sheet and good profitability, but if it is short on liquidity because its assets cannot readily be converted into cash then it will quickly run into problems. Positive working capital is required to ensure that a firm is able to continue its operations and that it has sufficient funds to satisfy both maturing short-term debt and upcoming operational expenses. Therefore, the effective forecasting, budgeting, planning, tracking, reporting and management of current assets and liabilities is critical and is what is referred to as working capital management.

The cash flow management watch list

The fundamental principles of working capital management are reducing the capital employed and improving efficiency in the areas of receivables, inventories, and payables.

Monitoring and management of "liquidity" of the moving parts of the business machine will be critical to success and could include any or all of:

- Day-to-day cash control
- Money at the bank
- Receipts
- Payments
- Short-term investments and borrowings
- Provision of bank accounts
- Deposit / withdrawal facilities
- Provision of information regarding bank accounts and positions
- Money transfers and collection services
- Investment facilities
- Financing facilities
- Pooling and netting

A BUSINESS OWNER OR MANAGER'S ABILITY TO FORECAST, budget, plan and monitor the flow of liquid resources will determine whether the business will exist and survive, thrive and prosper.

And – as the figure on page 48 so clearly illustrates, from a business owner or manager's perspective – your role as a principal in the business means you need cash management skills that are multi-dimensional and highly inter-dependent:

So why is cash flow management important?

There are many reasons why cash flow management is critical for the existence of your business:

Manage risks Your business might be making profits but you can be forced to exit or close up shop if you run out of the cash needed to pay debts or any of the other operational needs of the business.

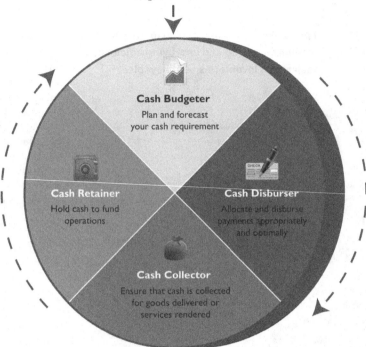

Cash Seeker
Source the funding from investors or lenders!

Cash Budgeter
Plan and forecast
your cash requirement

Cash Retainer
Hold cash to fund
operations

Cash Disburser
Allocate and disburse
payments appropriately
and optimally

Cash Collector
Ensure that cash is collected
for goods delivered or
services rendered

Figure 3: A SME investor/owner must play four critical cash flow management roles.

High levels of investments in current assets Investments in current assets form a significant part of overall investments. Therefore, managing working capital optimally will determine if the business is going to exist and survive, thrive and prosper.

Using current liabilities to fund a small business Most small businesses fund the operational aspects of their businesses through the current liabilities. Managing it optimally will determine whether you have a business or not!

High opportunity costs If you do not manage your working capital well, you might not have the requisite cash flow to take advantage of new growth opportunities, special discounts or increased customer demand. In other words, there is a huge opportunity cost if you do not manage your working capital effectively.

Ability to fund the running of a business Adequate working capital is required to ensure that your business is able to continue its operations and that you have enough funds to pay maturing short-term debts, meet the payroll, and have enough reserves for all the other ongoing operational expenses.

Increase overall free cash flow – Optimizing working capital results in availability of liquidity and thereby an improvement in your overall free cash flow which can be used to pay dividends to investors, to pay off debts and/or reinvest in the business.

Reduction in expenses – Optimal working capital management will lead to a significant reduction in inventory and borrowing costs, thereby further increasing profits and liquidity for "upside opportunity" investments and debt reduction.

Strengthened balance sheet gives increased stakeholder confidence A strengthened balance sheet for your small business will mean that your suppliers, customers, lenders, investors and even your employees will have increased confidence in your business. Countries across the world are currently fighting with this very same issue, with economic uncertainty forcing downgrades of their credit rating by the ratings agencies.

Strategies and tactics to optimize cash flow and/or liquidity

Before getting into the strategies and tactics that can be utilized to optimize cash flow management, it is important to understand the concept of "float". A float cost is any delay in the process of converting materials, labour and services to receipt of payment. Similarly, any delay in making payments to your suppliers will also give rise to float. Note that this is advantageous to a small business (up to a point).

So float is simply 'the difference between book cash and bank cash, representing the net effect of cheques in the process of clearing'. In other words, a float is time lost between a payer making a payment and a beneficiary receiving value.

So what are the strategies and tactics to manage business cash flow? In simplistic terms, cash flow can be as simple as making sure that that the business has enough profitable revenues. But one of the primary reasons a company often creates an environment of cash crunch is due to the lack of understanding of the "timing" element. Achieving higher revenues than expected sales is useless if you can't pay your bills during the time it takes for the proposition to be crafted and sold in the market.

"
Float is money we hold, but we don't own."
Warren Buffet,
investor

THERE IS NO ONE SINGLE SOLUTION TO MANAGING CASH FLOW, THOUGH EACH OF THESE WILL HELP YOU DEVELOP THE SKILLS THAT ARE NECESSARY:

1 **Manage owner and management compensation** For some small businesses, the owner's and management team's compensation is often a large portion of the business' expense – especially in the formative years of a business, the owner's draw can be a big burden on the cash flow of the business. That is why secondary incomes are valuable to the success of many small business ventures, especially in the early years.

2 **Manage overheads** Cut out excess overhead expenditures. Good spending discipline should keep unnecessary expenditures to a minimum, but good cash flow management should help to virtually eliminate excess overhead expenditures. Bad spending habits are often picked up when cash is plentiful.

3 **Cash flow information system and processes** You need to ensure that your financial information is maintained, stored and monitored in a manner that allows you to make the necessary adjustments for your small business. Therefore develop a good information system. Continual cash flow management is only as good as the information on which it is implemented. A record-keeping system that provides information useful to making decisions regarding cash inflows and outflows is essential.

4 **Planning and forecasting capabilities, processes and systems** A SME owner or manager will need to be able to plan and forecast optimally anticipated sales and expenditures. This is often overlooked.

5 **Rent or lease versus outright buy** Consider cash saving activities such as renting versus buying and used equipment versus new.

6 **Understanding cash flow peaks and troughs** You must know the timing and sizing of your cash in and cash out peaks!

7 **Limit overdue accounts due to the business** A small business must limit the money that is owed to it. In

other words, get people to pay their bills. Overdue accounts receivables can pull down a business. One way to address this problem is to keep credit current and at a minimum. This is often a bigger task than it may seem.

8 **Manage your credit risk** Caution should be taken when credit is first extended to customers.

9 **Give incentives for on-time and advance payment** Consider giving discounts for advance payments and incentives for payments made by the due date.

10 **Tight inventory management** Keep a close eye on inventory. Product sales and inventory management are complex issues that can be likened to the "chicken and egg syndrome". A business needs enough inventories to fill orders in a timely manner, but adequate sales are needed to minimize inventory. Inventory includes finished products held for future sales as well as raw materials held for future production. Both types of inventory represent cash that has been spent but that has not generated a return. Get rid of or sell inventory items that are just gathering dust at a discounted price.

11 **Timely billing and collections** Maintain tight reins on billing and collections. Because cash flow management is so closely tied to time (cash flows), the time lag between shipping finished products and receiving payment need to be minimized. The time lag issue must be aggressively addressed by collecting payments and sending invoices in a timely manner. Consider daily, weekly or fortnightly invoicing rather than monthly or bi-monthly invoicing.

12 **Optimally structuring payments to creditors** Consciously structure the payment of your bills. Electronic deposits and delayed payment of bills can improve cash flow problems. However, there is often a fine line between delayed payments and late payments. Crossing that line and incurring additional costs for late payments is normally not a good cash flow management procedure. Discounts on bills should be evaluated, i.e. consider discounts that offer less than the amount you save by delayed payments. All non-discount bills should be delayed as late as possible without compromising good relations. Do not hesitate to take advantage of credit offered by suppliers and feel free to negotiate for more favorable terms.

13 Issue monthly paychecks for employees Consider bi-weekly or monthly paychecks. Bi-weekly and monthly payrolls allow the business to hold onto money longer. It also allows for less frequent deposit of associated payroll and other taxes.

14 Monitor your customers' payment patterns Monitoring certain customers may provide insight into their payment schedule. A SME should consider dropping or implementing new payment procedures for customers who continually pay late.

15 Evaluate new customers from a cash-flow perspective When taking on new customers, consider implications on cash flow as part of the evaluation criteria, not just increased sales. Payment terms influence potential customers, but be cautious not to offer over-generous payment terms.

16 Automation and outsourcing Consider your operations and manufacturing if automation is better than using your own labour. Other considerations include considering giving a part of your operations to subcontractors versus manufacturing or servicing all aspects of the production or operations internally.

17 Differentiate your customers Segment and differentiate your cash and quick paying customers versus credit and late payers.

18 Business agility to adjust The business should have the capability, the willingness and readiness to make adjustments to the business and financial operations.

Summary

Cash flow management is one of the most fundamental issues that a business will have to grapple with. Mismanaging the timing of cash flows or misunderstanding their relevance will determine whether your business will thrive or perish. Remember that money makes money. More importantly, money today makes money tomorrow!

As an unnamed entrepreneur once famously said "the fact is that one of the earliest lessons I learned in business was that balance sheets and income statements are fiction, cash flow is reality".

So remember, "Happiness is a positive cash flow"!

NOTES

NOTHING WE DO IS MORE IMPORTANT THAN HIRING AND DEVELOPING PEOPLE: AT THE END OF THE DAY A BUSINESS RUNS ON ITS PEOPLE, NOT ON STRATEGIES.

HUMAN CAPITAL MANAGEMENT: SECRETS OF HIRING AND FIRING

Learning how to hire the right people and letting the wrong people go quickly

A company's employees really are its most important asset (and occasionally, admittedly, can be its biggest liability!) and they are not to be treated as disposable assets, with people hired and fired at will. The hiring and firing process calls for some sensitive management skills. Indeed, it is vitally important that due diligence and prudence is given to the job of hiring key employees. In fact, the hiring of employees might be among the most important decisions that any small business owner or investor will make on behalf of the company.

Equally, if a hiring mistake has been made, then it is of the utmost importance that the issue is dealt with swiftly and fairly.

This is not intended as a best practise guide in hiring or firing. The aim is simply to advice on stuff that is often overlooked based on personal experience, and the privilege and the opportunity of hiring across different countries, many highly talented folks.

There are common threads and characteristics in hiring that are worth watching out for. Similarly, it is useful to describe how to mitigate against situations that arise, if and when mistakes are made during recruitment. Most countries around the globe have laws that regulate and govern how businesses treat its employees. These need to be adhered to, of course. There are also some easy to use tools, various frameworks and a series of traits that can be identified and applied to ensure that risks are minimized.

Understanding the value of EPIC-based HR

No matter what job role you are seeking to fill, there are some basic and functional expectations that will be required of a potential candidate. These expectations could range from having a relevant professional degree, to a certain number of years of experience doing a relevant job. You would probably add additional expectations like the ability to communicate well, or the willingness to work flexible hours, and so forth. For good measure, you would in all likelihood add the requirement that a candidate be an excellent team player, be flexible, motivated, hardworking and so forth. In addition, for most management roles, you would expect a certain level of functional knowledge and intelligence, as well as analytical skills and demonstrable creative intelligence.

Of all the attributes that need to be considered during recruitment, it is easiest to miss out on a very important characteristic that will determine whether a potential candidate is going to succeed or not. It's called the EPIC factor, and it stands for a person who is an Emotionally and Practically Intelligent Candidate.

In the everyday work environment, especially in a challenging small business, emotions have a way of getting in the way of some very important relationships between the owner, a key manager, an employee, a key customer, a supplier or supporting staff. Therefore, it is important that employees possess and can apply their emotional intelligence – an ability to evaluate, determine, and perceive others around them. In most business situations, a conflict or disagreement is not generally over a certain strategy direction or a specific tactic or a task itself, but rather it pivots around the emotion of the moment. Emotional intelligence is often mistaken for a person who is able to control their temperament and does not get overtly angry. This is certainly not true.

One of the best descriptions of emotional intelligence is to compare it to an orchestra or band playing music to a lyric. The lyric itself is nothing without the music. You will never recall a lyric without the right recall of the accompanying music! In the same way, when a potential candidate interviewing for a job responds to a series of questions, their responses will include his or her cognitive ability to articulate the issue at hand.

> **Anyone can become angry – that is easy, but to be angry with the right person, to the right degree, at the right time, for the right purpose, and in the right way – this is not easy.**
>
> *Aristotle*

It is the emotion of the situation that provides the intonation, the sighs, gasps, gestures and animation. Without emotion we can expect only a robotic, matter of fact and boring discussion. In many senses emotion is like a beautiful picture or work of art with no one to admire it; it has instinctual, intellectual and creative aspects to it but there is no emotion. Or, take a house or building that is designed with brilliant architecture, but has no furniture or fittings and no occupants. The building is said to have no emotion.

So when you are hiring a key recruit, we need to be able to decipher how well the candidates combine their intellectual and creative capabilities to their emotional intelligence. It is a sure way to identify a candidate that can relate to others, versus someone who is drab and ineffective.

 Practical – Practical intelligence enables employees to fix problems realistically based on the environment or the situation that has been dealt for them. Is the candidate grounded with a good sense of reality, despite or in spite of all the bullishness or bearishness around them?

 Assertiveness – Can the candidate constructively state his or her own position, beliefs and take a stance without offending or belittling others. This is a critical requirement for leaders, and often goes hand in hand with an ability to challenge conventional wisdom or the status quo in a positive but reinforcing manner.

 Deliberate – Does the candidate appear impulsive or likely to take sudden or rash decisions based on a whim? Being deliberate in how a person responds to provocation, situations, or deals with business negotiations, and other scenarios could mean the difference between losses and profits for the business and for the individual.

 Flexibility – This is the ability of a person to adjust their responses, thoughts, emotions, actions and others to reflect the situation. This is especially critical when you are hiring a marketing or sales individual, as the job requires dynamic adjustment to the market environment, customers, competitors and other extenuating factors beyond any one's control. (Flexibility might not be an attribute you would expect of someone managing the company accounts!)

 Emotional self awareness – This is the ability of the candidate to recognise his or her feelings and emotions and relate and differentiate them. Candidates with high emotional intelligence will know what caused them and why. This is a critical requirement to enable successful workplace resolutions in areas of disagreement.

 Empathy – This is the ability to put oneself in someone else's shoe. The innate ability to relate, understand and empathize with another person's point of reference will lead to better workplace relationships with good levels of collaboration.

Figure 4: Primary characteristics to identify candidates with high emotional intelligence.

The EPIC-based interview process

As a small business owner or manager, you probably cannot hire expensive human resource consultants to test the power of these EPIC attributes, but each of them can easily be tested with scenarios related to your industry or business situation. Simply keep each of the recommended required attributes in mind and challenge the candidate in various scenarios. The key is to be prepared for the interview and once you have done four or five, it will come naturally to you.

The interview is not just about the functional, creative or intellectual capability of the candidate. These are easily verifiable. It is important to ensure a candidate would likely succeed in the often challenging business environment, and that they would make a real difference to the business! So, as well as the main attributes that we've already listed, there are others that will determine the overall emotional intelligence of a candidate. Some of the key ones that should be tested are:

- **Does the** candidate demonstrate a positive outlook and a sense of optimism?
- **Do they show** a sense of independence?
- **Are they** people oriented?
- **Do they** demonstrate self realization of their capabilities (their strengths and weaknesses)?
- **Do they** have an ability to work under stress?

> *"Always be smart enough to hire people brighter than yourself."*
> *John Lincoln, author*

Strategies and tactics for firing at will and without obstruction

Firing an employee is never easy. It can often be heart wrenching to say goodbye to an employee, and these emotional feelings can be exacerbated in these trying economic times. However, it often might mean the survival of your business and so it needs to be planned for. As a small business owner, you do not have the time or the appetite to be caught in a legal tussle with an ex-employee.

It is safest to assume that every termination will or might result in a legal suit against your company, and to mitigate against this there is a need to be mindful of some simple steps that stand as strategies and tactics to minimize the risk of legal action.

It is also important that any termination is labelled appropriately to avoid potential legal action and/or emotional over-reaction from your employee. Words like de-layering (when management is terminated) to right-sizing or reorganization are terms which should NOT be used when having to let employees go.

There are some specific labels that can rightly be applied to describe different circumstances that trigger termination:

- **Dismissal** This means that your employee's performance and/ or conduct were deemed unacceptable and unsatisfactory and failed to meet agreed performance objectives set in an appraisal. (In very special circumstances, suspension might be an alternative, before any decision is made to terminate permanently.)
- **Resignation** This means that your employee has voluntarily decided to part company with your business.
- **Retrenchment or lay off** This means that you have to terminate employment because of prevailing economic or trading reasons and that they will be rehired as soon as work is available.

When dealing with termination of employees, be deliberate and structured. You have no other choice, as the opportunity costs of time, money and morale of your employees are just too high!

WORDS LIKE DE-LAYERING (when management is terminated) to right-sizing or reorganization are terms which should NOT be used when having to let employees go.

John Lincoln, author

- DOCUMENTATION
- CONFIDENT
- RESPECT
- BE FAIR
- COMPENSATE FAIRLY
- BE TRANSPARENT
- HAVE A WITNESS
- OFFER REFERENCES

A checklist for compliance – safe and sensible steps towards fair and legal termination

1   **DOCUMENTATION** Have a well-documented file for every employee outlining any instance of misconduct, non performance, breach of contract, harassment or whatever reason you have, prior to terminating the employment of any employee, regardless of the reason.

2   **CONFIDENT** Exude confidence when you have to terminate an employee. If you are not confident, this could be misconstrued as unfair dismissal.

3   **RESPECT** Treat the employee with respect and dignity – even if he or she had stolen from you!

4   **BE FAIR** Exercise fairness. Your other employees are watching! You need them to succeed in your business after the event.

5   **COMPENSATE FAIRLY** Compensate your employees humanely, within the limits of affordability.

6   **BE TRANSPARENT** Be open, frank and candid when you have to deal with an employee whom you deem is no longer suitable for your business.

7   **HAVE A WITNESS** Have witnesses around you, when you are dealing with a termination. You do not want to be accused of harassment or anything worse.

8   **OFFER REFERENCES** If an employee has not been terminated for poor performance, breach of trust, violence or harassment, offer reference that will help them seek alternative employment.

NOTES

SECTION

PUTTING TOGETHER
THE BUSINESS
PROPOSITION

SIMPLY PUT, THE STRUCTURE OF A MARKET AFFECTS THE BEHAVIORS OF ALL THE COMPANIES THAT PLAY IN IT.

3.0

1.4

1.3

6

MARKETS, PRICING AND COMPETITIVE POSITIONING

Market structures, competitive positioning and the art of 'knowing your enemy'

There have been a lot of articles written about pricing, price wars and war gaming, and a lot has also been written on the strategies and tactics required to avoid and/or deal with a price war.

However, most of these articles are written in the context of large corporations who are often well funded and employ professional managers who have the requisite tools and capabilities to deal with a price war. There has been few to none written for small businesses. Although the guiding principles are the same for all "for profit" companies, some of the prescribed solutions are not apt for small businesses.

It is important for small businesses to define their industry structure and market trends and develop a purposeful pricing objective. Only then can small businesses determine their pricing strategy, let alone deal with, or avoid engaging in, a price war.

Strategic context of pricing

I have often wondered as to how much purposeful thought small business owners and SME marketers have given to their pricing strategy.

Pricing strategically is a core requirement that will determine the long term sustainability of a small business entity. Pricing is the purse string of any company. You mess with it and you are damned!

Most small businesses that I have interviewed do not consider aspects beyond cost-plus pricing to price their goods and services.

There are multiple pricing tools and frameworks that a small business owner or a SME marketer can deploy to sustain and win in the marketplace. We will discuss this in detail later. First, it is important to consider a small business' position in the marketplace, relative to the overall market.

Market structure and entry barriers

In discussing real world competition which most small businesses encounter daily, it is important to first focus and truly understands the market structure.

In essence, market structure is the number of companies in a market and the overall barrier to entry for others to enter in your space. For example, no small business can realistically aspire to be a utility or telecom operator as the initial investments are untenable and beyond the reach of most SMEs. In addition, meeting government and regulatory requirements requires investment in a battery of lawyers and regulatory experts. Additionally, hiring professional managers competent in the relevant technology or commercial aspects of the industry are certainly insurmountable for a small business investor.

Of course, most small business owners and SME marketers are smart and will not venture into such an endeavor. I am only attempting to illustrate an extreme example of what an entry barrier truly means.

IF THE ENTRY BARRIER IS LOW, THEN THE LONG TERM PROFIT PROSPECTS FOR A COMPANY ARE LOW AS WELL. So remember that when you develop your SME plan or your annual operating plans. Keep in mind that there are many others who can enter and disrupt your profits in your market space.

Measuring industry structure

First, here are some basics that small business owners must be aware of:

Perfect competition with an infinite number of companies and a monopoly are polar opposites. Monopolistic competition and oligopoly lie between these two extremes. Monopolistic competition is a market structure in which there are many businesses selling differentiated products. Oligopoly is a market structure in which there are a few interdependent firms.

Most global industry structures where small businesses operate fall almost entirely between monopolistic competition and oligopoly – perfectly competitive and monopolistic industries are nearly nonexistent.

Marketers in large companies often use one of two methods to measure the industry structure. They are the **concentration ratio** and the **Herfindahl Index**.

The concentration ratio is the percentage of industry output that a specific number of the largest companies have. The most commonly used concentration ratio is the four companies'

Figure 5: The structures that will determine the level of competitiveness of any industry.

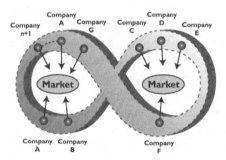

Perfect Competition

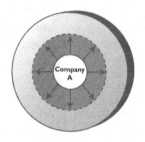

Monopolistic Market of One

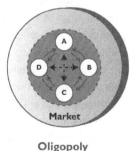

Oligopoly

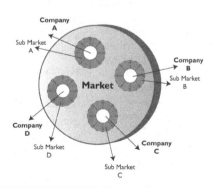

concentration ratio. The higher the ratio is, the closer the industry structure will be to an oligopolistic or monopolistic type of market structure.

The Herfindahl Index is an alternative method used by marketers to classify the competitiveness of an industry. It is calculated by adding the squared value of the market shares of all firms in the industry.

I personally prefer this method. There are two advantages of the Herfindahl Index. It takes into account all companies in an industry and it also gives extra weight to a single company that has an especially large market share. Also, the Herfindahl Index is the method used by the US Justice Department for allowing or disallowing mergers to take place. If the index is less than 1,000, the industry is considered competitive, whereby allowing a merger is actively considered.

Relevance of industry structure for business survival

By now you must be wondering why all this is important. Classifying the industry structure is important because structure affects a company's behavior. The greater the number of sellers, the more the likelihood that the industry structure in which a small business operates is competitive.

The number of businesses in an industry plays a role in determining whether small businesses explicitly take other companies' actions into account. In reality though (when there are many sellers as in monopolistic competition), they do not take into account their competitors' reactions.

If you are running a retail store or restaurant, this might not be very important for you. However, in many countries, there are many traders and distributors for large manufacturers or technology companies ranging from cell phones, computers and servers to sophisticated telepresence and medical equipment.

In addition, there are many boutique management and technology consulting companies competing with well-known global brands. I am sure those businesses that are competing in these market spaces can see the relevance of really understanding their industry structure.

A WORD ON MONOPOLISTIC COMPETITION
By now you must also be wondering as to why a hyper competitive industry structure is called monopolistic competition. It seems so counter intuitive. The "many sellers" characteristic gives monopolistic competition its competitive aspect; the need and capability for business proposition differentiation gives monopolistic competition its monopolistic aspect. SMB owners and SME marketers must ensure that their proposition is truly differentiated. And they must successfully communicate their unique value propositions to the market. This is a fundamental rule for any small business. Most small businesses operate in an environment where the entry barrier is very low and there are many sellers. Then, if there is no unique value proposition, or if the unique value proposition is not communicated well, the business is doomed to fail.

NOTES

LOOKING CLOSELY AT THE DETAILED END-TO-END EXPERIENCE OF THE CUSTOMER CYCLE IS A WINNING FORMULA – AND ONE THAT'S NEEDED TO DOMINATE THE MARKETPLACE AND DELIGHT YOUR CUSTOMERS.

THE PROPOSITION IS THE EXPERIENCE!

Create a totality of experience to get a satisfied customer

Entrepreneurs, marketers and businesses often talk about the customer value proposition. The term is popularly used to describe how a business' core product or service is designed to be used by the customer. This is only partly true, as it overlooks the need for a totality of experience approach which ought to be adopted by any business offering any proposition in a competitive environment. It is not just about how great the product is, or what great value for money it offers, or how it is promoted, or through which channels it will be sold – it is about the totality of the experience the customer is being sold.

A fantastic personal experience!

Anyone who has gone shopping in an Apple store will likely have experienced what can be called 'a totality of proposition experience' and here's a typical scenario.

At the end of December, I made my customary trip to Northern California to spend the holidays with my family. As so often happens, I was once again requested by one of my colleagues to pick up from the US one of the new release gadgets – this time a latest version MacBook Pro laptop, ahead of their availability in the region. I decided to make the purchase on a weekday after the holidays, as I wanted to avoid the mad shopping rush during the holiday period. I went into an Apple store in Walnut Creek in Northern California. I was greeted very pleasantly by all the sales associates who made eye contact with me. My focus normally would have been to get the best deal or the best value for money. The difference between this particular trip to the store and the previous ones was that I was not worried about the amount of money that I was going to spend. I was specifically requested to get a particular model for which I expected to be fully reimbursed by my colleague who had requested the MacBook Pro. So with no money worries, I focused my full attention on the workings of the store, and keenly observed its staff, surroundings, service and types of customers.

Under promised and over delivered

For starters, I felt the shop was conspicuously located in downtown Walnut Creek. It seemed to be a universal trait for Apple stores to be so strategically located. I have been to their stores in Tokyo, London, San Francisco, San Jose and others. For example, the store in Tokyo is located in the Ginza shopping district, considered one of the most expensive real estate addresses in the world!

My other observations were that the store was enticing and welcoming. Even if you had not planned to buy anything from Apple, I bet that passing through the street where the store was located would have drawn you in. The store was brightly lit and all the electronic gadgets were well placed with enough space for someone to walk around. The prices and the model numbers and specifications were clearly displayed. Although that particular store in Walnut Creek appeared to be busy, I got the sense that I would get immediate attention and service as the number of sales associates on hand seemed more than adequate. In other words I sensed that I would not be hassled nor would I be confused nor would I have had to wait long for someone to assist me.

I was approached by a young lady who introduced herself as Raven. She had a very bright and pleasant personality about her. She was courteous, professional and extremely knowledgeable. Since I knew exactly what I wanted, she did not hassle me with a lot of up-selling and cross-selling tactics that you would experience in other stores. She had what seemed to be a mobile gadget (an iPod Touch) through which she placed my order and transacted the payment. She inquired if I wanted a receipt which she offered by email as well as handing me a hard copy version. She showed me my email address displayed on her hand-held and which was already stored in the system (based on my previous purchases) and rechecked with me to confirm if she had the correct email address.

About two minutes after the order was placed, she logged on to a desktop system (which of course was a Mac) near her and confidently announced that the box would be delivered to me in about another three minutes. She explained that the stock was coming from upstairs hence the delay. I assured her that three minutes was not a delay at all. Imagine my surprise when I was handed the box roughly two minutes ahead of the promised three minutes. What an amazing experience – a classic case of under promising and over delivering. Just imagine that! My colleague was fully aware of the product and the model, and thought that Apple offered the best value for money. I walked into one of its stores and picked up the merchandise and had one of the best shopping experiences that I ever had (and I hate shopping)!

---

* *"The proposition is the experience. The experience forms the brand." This phrase was originally developed by Subhra Das, EVP Marketing and Customer Experience, du.*

When we examine the totality of proposition experience that Apple has designed for its customers in this way, it is abundantly clear that it is not just the technological superiority of its cool gadgets that Apple is marketing, but rather a perfect end-to-end customer experience.

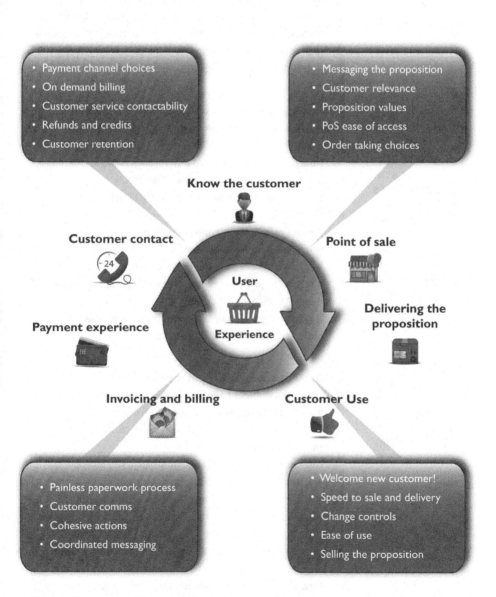

Figure 6: The customer value proposition is the totality of the end-to-end experience of the offer.

So what is the customer value proposition?

The customer value proposition is the totality of the end-to-end experience of the offer. This is a framework that we should seriously consider when designing the proposition. The proposition experience needs to account for every element of the customer lifecycle, from the time the customer gets to know of the product or service, to the time the customer leaves you. Let's consider what's involved:

HOW DO WE MAKE SURE THAT OUR SALES OR SERVICE AGENTS CAN EXPLAIN THE BENEFITS of our proposition, the relevant specifications and options available, and if it is suitable for a specific customer?

1 **Getting to know and understand the customer**
- **How do we make the proposition known** to potential customers?
- **How do our messages** and advertisements look to the customer, and how do they make them feel?
- **What is the visual experience** that the target customers will experience?
- **Are our messages friendly,** easy to understand and differentiated from our competitors?
- **How do we make sure the customer will only receive a call** / message if the proposition or service is appropriate and relevant to them?
- **How do we make sure that we make calls** /messages to customers only during appropriate times?

HOW DO WE MAKE SURE THE ORDER CAPTURE PROCESS takes less than x number of minutes using a single form which can capture all options and scenarios?

2 **Buying or purchasing point of sale**
- **Do our customers have easy access** to a sales channel of their choice to purchase the proposition?
- **What is the buying experience** in the store, through a website or a call centre?
- **Are our buying processes simple**, clear, non bureaucratic and easy to understand?
- **Are our prices transparent**, predictable and honest?
- **Are all our front-line staff fully trained** to explain and make the buying process easy?
- **What is the delivery time period?** Is it complicated? Is there a long wait for delivery of the proposition?
- **How do we get your customers to sign** a single contract with a single set of terms and conditions for a bundle of services?

- **How do we make sure** that once the customer has completed the purchase that our sales agent goes through a checklist of information to set the customer's expectations about next steps?
- **What is the delivery time period?** Is it complicated? Is there a long wait for delivery of the proposition?

3 Delivering the goods/activating or enabling the service

- **How quickly** can the customer start to use the service?
- **Is the signing on process** easy and simple?
- **How will the customer be informed** of any change to an appointment / service start date?

HOW DO WE MAKE SURE OUR CUSTOMER KNOWS where he or she can go to get information about the status of their order once it is placed?

4 The user experience

- **How do we welcome customers** once a service is activated and or enabled?
- **Is the proposition easy** to use?
- **Is it complicated** and cumbersome?
- **Is it confusing?**
- **Is it easy on our sales** and service staff to explain?

5 Invoicing and/or billing experience

- **Is the invoice easy to understand?** Is it confusing? Are bills delivered promptly?
- **How can we give** the customer a choice of billing options?

HOW CAN WE MAKE SURE THE ACTIVATION PROCESS FEELS UNIFIED and cohesive like the customer is receiving a single product, rather than a group of separate products stitched together?

6 Payment experience

- **How do we make sure** our customers have a choice of payment channels local to them and / or preferred by them?
- **How do we confirm** to a customer when their payment is received and when it is allocated to their account?

7 Customer contact experience

- **How can we make sure** customers are able to reach us?

8 Leaving

- **How does a customer leave our service** and get refunds and final bills?

Figure 7: Leveraging the four key marketing elements is critical to the design of the overall proposition.

Seize the opportunity and laugh your way to the bank!

Businesses large and small are guilty of limiting the allocation of resources to the important aspect of proposition lifecycles, and this might be a tremendous opportunity for you to differentiate for competitive advantage.

Planning and thinking seriously through the end-to-end experience of the customer cycle is a winning formula that is required to dominate the marketplace and delight your customers. It calls for continuous scrutiny and constant refinement and will pay off handsomely in the end.

You will not only be delighting your customers, but could be laughing all the way to the bank!

NOTES

THE BRAND
PERSONIFIES
THE PERCEIVED
VALUE OF YOUR
PROPOSITIONS
VERSUS YOUR
COMPETITORS.
IT IS THE IMAGE
THAT YOU
PORTRAY TO
THE OUTSIDE
WORLD.

THE EXPERIENCE FORMS THE BRAND*

Why brand strategy and branding critically matters for SMEs!

A LOGO ALONE IS NOT A BRAND!

Top of mind awareness

Have you ever wondered why some brand names are synonymous with their product or service category? Have you also wondered as to why some brand names come first in your mind when you are thinking or considering a certain product or service category? Go ahead: pick a category ranging in products, say, from copiers to phones. Which brand names come first in your mind? Why did that particular brand come to your mind?

It is because the companies who own their brand names have a purposeful branding strategy and have committed significant resources to ensure that their branding achieves top of mind awareness from their existing and potential customers. I will discuss later, in detail, as to why this is critical.

---

* *"The proposition is the experience. The experience forms the brand." This phrase was originally developed by Subhra Das, EVP Marketing and Customer Experience, du.*

A logo or a company name is not branding!

Most SME owners or small business managers think of branding as fluffy, useless stuff and a sheer waste of time and money. This is a fallacy that they must correct immediately. If the strategic intent of a business is to grow and sustain, that business will have to think of branding more seriously than how most are approaching it today. This chapter is not a discussion as to the advertising or communications tactics and media used to communicate. There are enough books and blogs written on this.

The choice of media and the amount you spend depends on your company's financial resources. Branding is a lot more than just about communications through different media.

A BRAND IS THE ESSENCE OF YOUR SMALL BUSINESS. It encapsulates your core products and services, your reputation and the total experience promise you make to your customers. The brand personifies the perceived value of your propositions versus your competitors. It is the image that you portray to the outside world – not just your customers but all your stakeholders, including your employees, suppliers, partners and funders.

* *"The proposition is the experience. The experience forms the brand." This phrase was originally developed by Subhra Das, EVP Marketing and Customer Experience, du.*

So, what is a brand?

Whether you know it or not, almost every product, service, business, public personality, and company has been branded. Many small businesses (and large company executives too) use the terms visual identity, corporate identity, brand identity and branding interchangeably. Branding is a broader marketing effort than visual identity since it often involves naming, communications and advertising, as well as promotion.

Many think of a brand as a logo, proprietary name for a product, service, or group; however, in reality, a brand is the sum total of all characteristics and assets of a brand name product, service, or group that differentiates it from the competition, as well as the perception of the brand by the public.

In other words, there are several key components of an overarching branding effort or program, beginning with a logo and visual identity through interactive experiences, package design, corporate communications, promotional design and advertising.

A brand is also the mind share that you occupy in your customers' minds based on the totality of the experience that they have experienced with your company, across all or any touch points. These touch points are not just the obvious marketing collateral, business cards and press releases. It could range from how they get to know about your business and propositions, to whom, how and where they interacted with to buy the products or service to using the product or service and so forth.

The purpose of branding

Before I start on the purpose of branding, there are a few definitions that you must be aware of:

- **A brand** is a unique or proprietary name for a business, product, or service. It is the totality of all characteristics and assets of a brand name product, service, or group that helps customers differentiate your small business from your competitors, as well as your customers and the general public's perception of your brand.

- **Branding** is not brand strategy but is the development and the execution process of creating a brand, brand name, and visual identity for all your internal and external communications and touch points.

- **A brand strategy** is the concept, framework and plan providing guidelines for all your internal and external brand executions across all touch points.

- **A brand experience** is the experience of ALL your stakeholders and not just your customers at every touch point through which a stakeholder (customers, employees, suppliers, lenders, partners and shareholders) comes into contact with your brand or company.

IN ESSENCE, THE BRAND IS ALSO THE PERSONALITY AND SOUL OF YOUR COMPANY by which your employees are hired to how your customers perceive you. It is NOT only the soul and personality either but also your company's philosophy by which you think, define, prospect, interact and serve your customers.

What is brand strategy?

A brand strategy defines the brand's personality and promise. The brand enables and differentiates your company through your brand positioning. Your small business brand strategy is the core strategic underpinning of branding, uniting all planning for every visual and verbal application. The brand strategy defines the brand's personality and promise. The brand strategy also codifies the brand essence of your small business and tactical execution and implementation within your company. The brand design makes the strategy real and alive and gives brands their distinctive look and feel. The brand strategy will help your small business brand to identify and communicate a core value, quality or differentiator that can become the construct or position, for SME brands to own against its competitors.

In other words, the small business brand strategy is how you are formulating, defining, conceiving, creating, and positioning your brand in the marketplace to achieve differentiation, relevance, engagement and resonance with your current and potential customers and all your stakeholders.

Why is a brand strategy important for your small business?

Nothing can better help your business to grow and flourish than a successful brand strategy. Here's why you MUST have a well-defined plan:

IDENTITY
A PURPOSEFUL BRAND STRATEGY WILL DEFINE THE OUTWARD EXPRESSION OF YOUR SMALL BUSINESS BRAND, including your small business name and visual appearance. This is important as the brand's identity is its fundamental means for your customers to recognize your brand. A consistent visual identity will help your small business brand to differentiate from your competitors.

AWARENESS Branding helps your customers to spontaneously recall your company or helps your customers to recognize that you exist.

EXPERIENCE A consistent brand strategy will help your SME to create a brand in the minds of your customers through your customers' experiences across all your touch points. The intentional customer experience has to be defined and be consistent for your customers to create your brand in their minds.

ESSENCE A brand strategy helps your SME business to express its promise in the simplest, most single-minded terms. For example, Ritz Carlton = Excellence in service; Mercedes Benz = German engineering quality. However, it is not something that is whimsical as it has to be rooted in a core customer need.

PERSONALITY Your brand strategy will help your small business customers to attribute or give your brand human personality traits such as fun, warmth, innovative, cool, etc. This perceived personality of your brand by your customers is how you differentiate yourself in the minds of your customers. Brand personality does not happen overnight. You as a small business owner should have a long term view as to how you want your brand to be perceived by your customers. These personality traits will inform the brand behavior through all your external and internal communications, packaging etc., and through the people who represent your small business brand – you and your employees.

HARMONIZATION A purposeful brand strategy will ensure that all your products and services, especially if you have a broad range of services or products, will have a consistent name, visual identity and, ideally, positioning across all the markets that you operate in.

IMAGE A consistent branding derived from a deliberate brand strategy will create a consistent net "out-take" of your brand for your customers. This image is derived based on the experiences of your products or services and are informed impressions as to how well your small business meets your customers' expectations. For potential customers your small business brand's image in their minds will be based upon uninformed impressions, attitudes and beliefs.

VALUES A purposeful brand strategy will help you define and design the code by which your small business brand lives. The brand values act as a benchmark to hire as well as measure behaviors and overall performance.

ARCHITECTURE A brand strategy helps your small business to define its brand architecture. In other words, it helps your business to determine how it structures and names the brands within its portfolio. This is important for a small business owner or investor having a diverse portfolio of goods, services or businesses. There are three main types of brand architecture systems:

- **Monolithic** where the group name is used on all products and services offered by your holding company.

- **Endorsed** where all sub-brands are linked to your group brand by means of either a verbal or visual endorsement.

- **Freestanding** where the group brand operates merely as a holding company, and each product or service is individually branded for its target market.

POSITIONING
A PURPOSEFUL BRAND STRATEGY HELPS YOU TO HAVE A DISTINCTIVE POSITION IN YOUR MARKETPLACE to enable your customers in your target market to identify and differentiate your small business brand. Positioning doesn't just involve the logos or other visual identities alone, but involves leveraging and the careful manipulation of every element of the marketing mix, to deliver a superior and differentiated proposition to your customers.

ASSOCIATIONS A brand strategy encompasses your customers' feelings, beliefs and knowledge that existing and potential customers have about your SME brand. These positive (or negative) associations are derived as the sum total of all their experiences across all touch points. These experiences must be consistent with the brand positioning and the basis of differentiation.

COMMITMENT A structured, well defined and purposeful brand strategy will increase the commitment of your customers to your propositions in the market. If your customers' commitment to your brand is high, the propensity for repurchase and/or reuse is very high. The level of commitment indicates the vulnerability of your SME brand and is a good indicator of the probability of competitors poaching your customers.

VALUE OR EQUITY Having a purposeful brand strategy will increase the long term value of your small business through the increased brand equity derived from the sum of all distinguishing qualities of a brand, drawn from all relevant stakeholders. This will facilitate personal commitment from you and demand of you for the brand; these differentiating thoughts and feelings make the brand valued and valuable and, therefore, your small business more valuable.

EXTENSION A consistent, structured and purposeful brand strategy will help your small business to leverage the equity and values of the brand to take the brand into new business opportunities, partnerships and newer markets/sectors.

- A brand name is the verbal identity of your small business – a proprietary name – and coupled with a tagline or descriptor, it becomes the verbal signature.

- Without question, the brand name is the main point of reference to your business and is the main verbal marketing tool.

- **Naming your small business brand involves many important considerations.**

  What does the name mean to your employees and customers?

  What type of spirit or personality should it convey to all your stakeholders?

  How will people react to it?

  What does the name mean in a specific language across cultures?

- **There are several categories of name types that are more or less appropriate for any small business brand.**

  Founder's name: named after the company's founder(s)

  Explanatory: named to best explain or describe the product or service

  Expressive or invented: names that are constructed to have a certain panache or sound

  Allegorical or symbolic: names that express their nature through an allusion to an allegory or a symbol

  Acronym: a brand name formed from the initials or other parts of several names or words

- **There are many ways to make your small business brand name effective. They can be:**

  Distinctive

  Extendable

  Memorable

  Long-lasting

  Purposeful

  Legally owned

How to correctly name a brand

PAY ATTENTION TO THE VITAL DESIGN DEVELOPMENT STAGE

- Based on the strategy, name and construct for your small business brand, the visualization and composition begin during design development. You, as the small business owner, will need to consider brand differentiation, brand promise, and branding applications and media.

DIFFERENTIATION THROUGH LOOK AND FEEL

As part of the design solution, your small business brand's unique personality is established and communicated through its "look and feel" and expressed through the particulars of the visualization and composition, including

- **color palette**
- **characteristics and qualities of lines, shapes, and textures**
- **typeface**
- **and any other visual elements**

The brand look and feel is a visual "attitude" that differentiates your small business brand from the competition, making it unique, distinctive, memorable, and relevant to its audience.

Your small business brand's look and feel should define its individual character and be synonymous with your brand. It should not, in any way, be generic, and should definitely not be similar to your competitors' look and feel.

"Success means never letting the competition define you. Instead you have to define yourself based on a point of view you care deeply about."

Tom Chappell, businessman extraordinaire

Reiteration of branding and differentiation

Efficacy

In a hyper competitive marketplace, relevant and engaging branding can ensure efficacy for your small business if you can deliver quality products and services.

Equity

Not only does branding distinguish your small business, it builds equity, and therefore the value of your company.

Mind share

You have to differentiate your products and services in the minds of your customers. This is imperative in a glutted and highly competitive market.

Product parity

Very few small business products and services offer unique benefits, and often offer similar or identical functions as their competitors. Branding helps to differentiate in markets where parity of products and services exist.

Verbal differentiators

An optimal branding differentiates your small business brand by offering two main verbal differentiators – the brand name which should be proprietary to your small business and a tagline, a slogan or short distinctive phrase.

Visual identifier

I don't mean to make light of the importance of your logo as it is one of the key visual identifiers vis a vis your competitors, for your small business.

Quality

Branding helps you pre-empt your competitors by claiming ownership or benefit of a quality by establishing your small business brand in your customers' mind as the primary possessor of that quality; in other words, it is the positioning of your small business brand in the market place against the competition. A structured branding approach enables your small business to "claim" ownership of a benefit or quality before anyone else does. However you will have to express that construct through the visual and verbal identity.

In other words, branding is not fluffy, useless stuff but rather it helps your small business to differentiate your products and services in a crowded brand world.

Figure 8: How brand strategy and branding helps your SME to differentiate in the marketplace.

A brand for the company is like a reputation for a person. You earn reputation by trying to do hard things well."

Jeff Bezos, founder, Amazon.com

> If you don't get noticed, you don't have anything. You just have to be noticed, but the art is in getting noticed naturally, without screaming or without tricks."
>
> *Leo Burnett, advertising pioneer*

Summary

Your small business can build a strong brand if you can build loyalty among your customers. To build loyalty, your customers have to be aware of your brand. To claim top of mind awareness, you must differentiate your brand with a distinct visual and verbal identity. Your communications across all touch points have to be relevant to the target market. Your small business will have to define the intentional customer experience across all touch points with a clear understanding of how your customers' relationship with your brand can develop, from basic awareness to intense loyalty. Identifying where your customers are on this "journey to loyalty" is a crucial first step towards developing an effective marketing strategy for your small business.

To build a stronger brand, you need to know much more than the size and shape of your market and customer base. You need to understand how well your brand is performing in terms of winning loyalty.

You need to identify and track the competitive strengths and weaknesses that may be helping or hindering your brand in the battle for increased loyalty. In other words, the experience of your customers and all your stakeholders across all touch points is the brand. It certainly is NOT just about your logos and collaterals.

I want to leave you with 3 memorable quotes that succinctly put brand strategy and branding in perspective. At least it did for me.

Indeed the experience is the brand and the brand is the experience!

NOTES

MOST SMALL BUSINESSES AND SME OWNERS OFTEN MISTAKENLY REQUEST THE GOOD FOLKS FROM THE FINANCE FUNCTION TO SET THE PRICING FOR THEIR PROPOSITIONS. THIS IS A GRAVE MISTAKE.

PRICING STRATEGIES AND TACTICS FOR YOUR BUSINESS

Asking the right questions and locating the correct objectives of your pricing policy must be a priority

I t is vitally important for small businesses to get their pricing strategy right, before they can even think about a price war. SMB owners and SME marketers must carefully reflect on the real objectives of a market's pricing approach. There could be many reasons and objectives for a pricing move. Before we summarize the different profit objectives, it is important for small businesses to consider the trends in the market:

NINE QUESTIONS YOU MUST ASK BEFORE YOU DECIDE ON PRICING

1 Is there a flood of new propositions or model introductions in the market?
2 Is there an increased availability of bargain and generic brands in the market?
3 Are your competitors using price cutting as a strategy to maintain or regain market share?
4 Is there a general decline in consumer confidence (following events such as a political upheaval, terrorist attack, stock market crash etc)?
5 What stage is your proposition in the product's life cycle? Is it mature?
6 What is the competitive intensity in your market space?
7 What is your distribution strategy? Direct, indirect or hybrid sales approach?
8 What is your promotion or communications strategy?
9 What is the perceived quality of your proposition relative to your competitors?

Pricing objectives

Only after truly understanding their industry structure and market trends should small business owners and SME marketers consider and define their profit objectives.

- **Survival mode** – Are you just trying to survive and generate enough cash flow to remain in business?
- **Maintaining status quo** – Are you trying to maintain the status quo in the hope of avoiding a price war?
- **Cost recovery** – Are you seeking only partial cost recovery?
- **Quality leadership** – Is the small business seeking to signal a higher quality of the proposition?
- **Maximize current profits** – Is the SME seeking to maximize current profits?
- **Maximize current revenues** – Are you seeking to maximize current revenues and not the profits?
- **Maximize quantity** – Is your small business seeking to maximize quantity to recover long term costs?
- **Maximize profit margins** – Is the SME seeking to maximize profit margins knowing well the impact it has on the demand for the small business' products and services?

Now that you have a systematized view of the industry structure, the prevailing trends in the market and a purposeful pricing objective, it is time to reflect on what your strategic pricing approach should be.

Strategic pricing

There are many different types of pricing strategy that a small business owner or marketer can follow:

1   **Penetration pricing** The strategic objective is to quickly increase sales and gain momentum. For example, a small business distributor of consumer electronics goods might use this strategy to pre-empt a competitor launch which is some time away.

2   **Skimming pricing** The small business owner can set an initial high price and then gradually lower the price to make the proposition available to a wider market. The strategic objective is to skim profits off the market layer by layer. If you are a small software games developer or a distributor of toys or consumer electronics, skimming might be an excellent approach, if the main festive buying season is some time away.

3   **Competition pricing** The objective is to set a price that compares with the competitors' rates. In reality, a small business has three options: price lower, price the same or price higher.

4   **Product line pricing** The strategic objective is to price different products within the same product range at different price points. Example: hotel room rates.

5   **Bundle pricing** The SME can bundle a group of products at a reduced price. Common methods are to buy one and get one free. Other creative methods could include offering a set menu for restaurants, bundling complementary products like movie tickets and popcorn etc.

6   **Bucket pricing** In this pricing method, SMEs can offer large volumes or buckets of the same proposition for a fixed period commitment. A small business restaurant owner, hotelier or a transportation company can offer bucket pricing for a fixed fee on a monthly or annual basis.

7   **Psychological pricing** When pricing their propositions, SMB owners and SME marketers should consider the psychology of price and the positioning of the price within the marketplace. This is why you see a lot of $1.99 or $999 type of pricing.

8 **Premium pricing** The strategy is to set the price high to reflect the exclusiveness or the premium quality of the product. This is commonly used by retailers and sellers of premium goods and services.

9 **Optional pricing** In this pricing approach, the SME can sell optional goods or services along with a main proposition.

10 **Cost-based pricing** In this pricing approach, the SME takes into account the cost of sales and distribution and then applies a markup for the intended profit, before deciding on a final pricing framework.

11 **Cost-plus pricing** Here, the SME adds a percentage to costs as a profit margin to decide on a market pricing decision.

12 **Loyalty-based pricing** In this pricing approach, the proposition offered uses all of the above pricing methods, and then prices are discounted to entice commitment, and therefore loyalty, over a period.

" *I recently met the owner of a company that sells software over the Internet to SMEs. Prior to this endeavor, this gentleman was a very senior manager in a well-known global software giant. What baffled me the most was his pricing strategy.*

In my mind, he truly lacked an understanding of his customer needs and affordability. More importantly, he failed to understand that his potential customers did not have the necessary cash flow for such upfront investments and that his only value proposition, relative to his other competitors in the market, was offering his customers an OPEX model versus a CAPEX model. "

Avoid the pricing pitfall

Most small businesses and SME owners often mistakenly request the good folks from the Finance function to set the pricing for their propositions. This is a grave mistake.

The pricing strategy and the tactics have to be set by someone who understands the needs of the customers, customer perceptions, and market conditions and has a well-rounded view of the business.

Of course, as pricing is the purse string of your business, it is important that there be checks and balances. This means that any pricing strategy or tactic will need to be validated and approved by independent functions like Finance or Accounting. However, they should not set the pricing.

The importance of perceived value

Small businesses need to know that most customers buy their propositions not for their features (eg a phone) or their specific functionalities (eg camera pixels), but rather for the perceived benefits that the propositions deliver.

Features and functions – which are often the focus of product design specifications – are simply the envelop wrap for delivering the benefits that are desired by customers.

Customer perceptions are critically important! A proposition may pass the required functional criteria, but a small business only gets credit if the customers recognize (i.e. "perceive") that the product delivers the benefits.

Similarly, potential customers make purchase decisions considering a proposition's perceived price. That is, how much a customer thinks that a product should cost him/her. These perceptions may or may not accurately reflect reality.

KEEP IN MIND THAT THE PERCEIVED VALUE is either the difference between the perceived benefits that a product delivers and its perceived price, or the ratio of the perceived benefits and the perceived price.

Comparison of perceived values

SMEs should know that customers often decide that they will not pay above a certain price. They make these choices by comparing across a set of reference propositions, explicitly or implicitly, for unscientific perceptual benchmarking (eg this type of product should cost roughly this amount). For example, the cost of an Apple iPad versus a Blackberry Playbook.

Customers also compare among substitutable products that may be directly or indirectly competitive. For example, Colgate and Close Up toothpastes are directly competitive. Colgate toothpaste and mouthwash are indirectly competitive (since both serve a different purpose and are dental hygiene products – unless someone only uses mouthwash for their dental hygiene!).

NOTES

PRICE WARS IN GENERAL ARE NOT GOOD FOR THE COMPANIES INVOLVED. THE LOWER PRICES REDUCE PROFITABILITY AND CAN THREATEN A SME'S SURVIVAL.

HOW DO YOU ENGAGE IN A PRICE WAR?

All war is deception: when to engage in a price war, its tactics and the fallout

Much has been written about pricing, price wars and predatory pricing, and there have been many more column inches devoted to the strategies required and tactics best applied when dealing with or avoiding a price war. There are many case examples to be found involving a variety of companies and a range of industries:

- **PepsiCo, Coke and Nestle** are some of the big name companies that have slashed prices on bottled water at various times and different rounds of a price war.
- **All the leading brand video game console manufacturers** have engaged periodically to try lure gamers with cut-price platforms.
- **Walmart and Amazon** have fought a well-publicised price war over the on-line book market.
- **Credit card issuers** almost routinely fight price wars over 0% balance transfer cards.
- **Telecom operators** will campaign against each other, with claims of the highest internet speed at the lowest price.

Price wars are not solely the province of large corporations though, and they impact SMBs and smaller businesses to varying degrees, depending on their industry structure, current market trends and the company's pricing objectives.

What is a price war?

Price war is a term used in marketing to indicate a state of intense competition followed by a series of price reductions. One player will lower its price; the others will lower their prices to match. If one of them reduces its price again, a new round of reductions will start. This is what is commonly referred to as an escalating price war.

Price wars in general are not good for the companies involved. The lower prices reduce profitability and can threaten a SME's survival. The small businesses cannot compete and must close. In the long term, your customers are the losers too. If there is less competition, prices tend to increase, sometimes going higher than before the price war started (the US cable industry is one example).

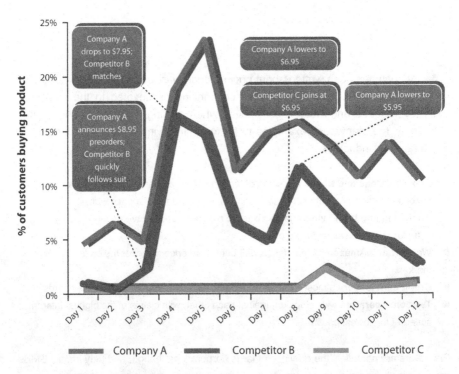

Figure 9: A typical example of an escalating price war.

What triggers a price war?

Price wars are often triggered due to the following reasons:

- **Excess capacity** – Excess inventory in the market arising from low demand (due to adverse economic conditions), excessive production and new entrants adding further capacity in the market. All these events are sure triggers for the start of a price war among all the players. This is an established reality in Dubai, for example, where real estate and rental costs have plummeted recently.

- **Comparable products** – When there are a large number of comparable products in the market, it typically leads to a price war. The sector of consumer electronics, with its wide option of televisions, mobiles and laptops, is a good example.

- **Price elasticity** – If certain players in the market believe that elasticity can be extracted from certain segments – that is, if a competitor believes that pricing is generally high in the market and that more demand could be generated from certain segments by lowering prices – then this becomes another trigger for a price war. This is the reason why a swarm of mobile phone and PC manufacturers are racing to serve the unmet needs of the bottom of the pyramid. Another good example is the introduction of the Tata Nano car in India. Now we have Bajaj, a famous manufacturer of scooters and bikes, also entering the fray.

- **Incompetent management** – An unnecessary price war could be triggered by some managers to meet their short term targets. These incompetent managers give no consideration to the long term value destruction in the market Managers are often measured on yearly achievement of targets. Lowering prices is a surefire way to meet short term targets.

- **Desperation** – You could also expect a price war when a large established player loses market share to a new entrant by remaining non-competitive. Conversely, a price war could be triggered by a small business desperately trying to generate incremental cash flow to survive.

- **High fixed cost structure** – Price wars could start when competitors keep a close eye on volume to reduce the average unit of fixed cost contribution, based on the belief that discounts will generate volumes to cover their fixed costs. This is common when businesses have invested a lot in fixed assets like plant, machinery and equipment.

- **Low degree of industry change** – A price war can happen when some players perceive that the industry structure is stale and not evolving fast enough. Some player will then start a price war as they rightly or wrongly see an opportunity to disrupt the marketplace.

- **Low switching costs for customers** – If you are in an industry where the switching costs for a customer is low, then there will be an attempt by your competitors to try and poach your customers with a price based proposition. This is very common for the Fast Moving Consumable Goods (FMCG) sector.

Dealing with the threat of a price war – considering the options

Non price options

I Compete on quality and differentiation

If your proposition is already differentiated, ensure that you communicate the incremental features, benefits and value of your differentiated offer.

Most SMEs do not have the luxury of tweaking their tangible features in their proposition. However, there are ample opportunities to address the intangible aspects like superior service, deep relationships, offering special and bespoke packaging and bundling with other products and services.

This is important because if you do not have the requisite differentiation, it would behoove you to offer incremental service packages at low or no cost to compete on your main proposition.

For example, in times of economic recession, hotels often drop their prices. But the Ritz-Carlton never competes on price. They are able to do this as they have positioned and delivered their proposition as the "Gold Standard".

2 Communicate weakness and threat to your customers

Another option that SMEs have is to communicate to your buyers the inherent risk in buying a low priced – meaning low quality – proposition. Small businesses should also communicate to their customers the inherent long term risks to your customers' business if you, as the SME, is forced to exit the market.

This is an important strategic move as customers will need to be told that prices will eventually rise as all the smaller players are forced out of the market.

3 Form strategic partnerships or alliances

You can offer exclusive deals with your main proposition, created through partnerships and alliances. For example, if you are a small business car dealer you could enter into a special deal with a major electronics distributor or airlines to offer exclusive deals and miles for any new car purchased through your dealership.

Reveal your strategic intentions and capabilities

You should reveal your strategic intention to your competitors. This could include your intent not to start a direct price war by maintaining your prices.

This is important as there are many incompetent folks who are trigger happy to reduce prices.

Conversely, this could include your intention to match with everyday low prices, just in case a desperate competitor is stupid enough to start a price war. (Frankly, this might not be tenable and sustainable for most small businesses; but this is a viable option for distributors who have the support of their principals).

As a small business distributor of some large established brands, you can also make sure that your competitors know that your costs are low (if it is low). This will effectively warn your competition about the potential consequences of starting a price war with you.

If you are reducing costs, be warned that it will adversely diminish your customers' perceptions of quality and could well trigger an unprofitable price war.

Price options

1 Deploy indirect pricing tactics addressing perceived value

SMEs have the option of initiating perceived pricing tactics such as segmented pricing, multiple-part pricing, volume discounts, pay per use pricing, bundling, bucketing, loyalty pricing and so on. These pricing moves allow the small business marketers to selectively cut prices for only those segments of the target customers are under competitive threat from a price war.

i.   Segmented pricing is when two prices are set for one product without a difference in production or distribution costs.

ii. Multi-part pricing is commonly used by providers of such services as car rentals, prescription drug plans and mobile phones. The general structure of these pricing schemes is a fixed access fee which sometimes entitles customers to a certain level of product use, a variable fee for additional use, and still another fee for add-on features that are priced individually and/or as bundles.

iii. Volume discount indicates a decrease in price when the buyer acquires a particularly large quantity of a product. A seller may offer a volume discount to entice buyers to conduct business with him/her. This reduces the profit that a seller makes on the individual product but it allows him/her to make a large sale quickly and receive the proceeds in short order.

iv. Pay per use pricing does what it says: you pay only for what you use. There is no minimum fee.

v. Bundling is the practise of joining related products together to sell them as a single unit. So, customers who want one must buy both. A more subtle form of bundling is to give customers who buy products together a discount.

vi. Loyalty pricing comes into effect when customers actually earn discounts. For example, multi-step quantity discounts, price guarantees etc.

2 Limit the theater of operations in the price war

Rather than responding with an all-out price cut (which a SME invariably could potentially lose), one option is to change your customers' choices.

This means that a small business can limit the adverse impacts to a narrow segment/channel/sector/region.

For example, if you are in the retail, hospitality or transportation industry, you can avoid across-the-board price cuts and localize a price war to a limited theater of operation – that is, limit the war to some sectors and/or regions.

Alternatively, if you are running a B2B business supplying across all vertical markets, you could limit the war to a specific channel focused on a specific vertical.

If you are a distributor of consumer electronics representing major Original Equipment Manufacturers (OEMs) in the region, you almost always have a high end, medium end and a low end proposition to cater to the price sensitivity across different segments.

Cutting prices across all the segments is a silly move as most buyers of high-end consumer electronics are price inelastic. Rather than diluting the premium quality of your proposition for the high end and medium end targets, you can have a low priced option, an alternate package or even an alternate brand, to target the low end.

When would you engage in a price war?

Small businesses are strongly advised against starting a price war. However, sometimes you are compelled to do so. I would recommend that you ask the following questions before starting or engaging in a direct price war:

- **Do your principal investors** and suppliers have deep pockets to survive and sustain a price war?

- **Do you have excess capacity** or inventory that must be sold?

- **Is your core business** or proposition, the very essence of your survival, being threatened by a price war from a large competitor?

- **Can a retaliatory price cut sway** a large portion of customers back to you?

- **Is there untapped elasticity** in certain segments in the market that you serve? Is there a large segment of price sensitive customers who have not adopted your proposition due to affordability factors?

Long term implications of a price war

CHANGES IN BEHAVIOR OF CUSTOMERS – Price wars change the behavior of customers. They teach customers to anticipate lower prices and often force them to defer their purchase in anticipation of low prices.

PERCEIVED QUALITY OF THE BRAND SUFFERS – The image and positioning of your brand will suffer. Your price cutting efforts will, in the long term, affect the perceived quality of your propositions. Often, not only the perceived value of a single affected proposition will suffer, but this has the potential for the perceived value of ALL your propositions in the market to suffer.

TRIGGERS RETALIATION FROM AFFECTED PLAYERS – A price cut will eventually wake up a giant who has been hurt. Once you harm the interest of other players, you should expect them to retaliate.

NEVER WAKE A SLEEPING GIANT. Let sleeping giants sleep.

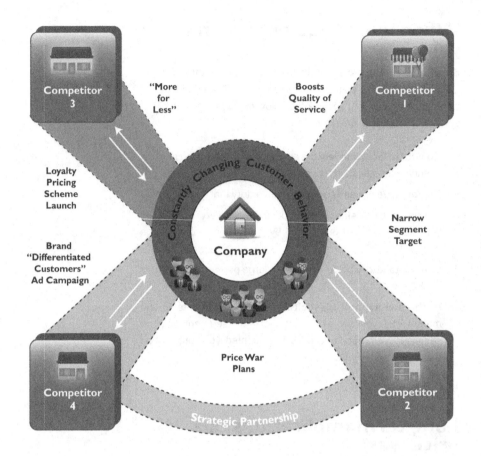

Figure 10: Leveraging price alone is NOT the only option to engage in a price war.

Summary

In my long career across different countries and companies, I have been involved in, or have led the start of, a price war. I can certainly assure you that in the long term it was counterproductive and the industry lost as a whole.

In this context, I would like to leave you with three thoughts from my all-time favorite military strategist. Most of you must have heard of Sun Tzu, the ancient Chinese military strategist who wrote the treatise, The Art of War. His advice:

- *"Know the enemy and know yourself; in a hundred battles you will never be in peril."*

- *"All warfare is based on deception."*

- *"Your aim must be to take all-under-Heaven intact. Thus your troops are not worn out and your gains will be complete. This is the art of offensive strategy."*

Keep these three principles from this ancient strategist in mind before you start or engage in a price war!

NOTES

SECTION

GO-TO-MARKET
STRATEGIES

THE TRICK TO MANAGING A SALES OPERATION IS KNOWING RELIABLY THE NUMBER OF CUSTOMERS AND THE POTENTIAL DEAL SIZE IN EACH STAGE OF THE SALES CYCLE.

THE ART OF SALES LEADERSHIP AND MANAGEMENT

Defining sales performance and identifying the key factors that drive superior performance

Every business that sells product or services to other businesses or consumers is required to have a robust sales function. So how can we define sales performance and what are the elements that make for a well-oiled sales machine? Sales performance is often defined as the product of a sum of different moving parts, which can be challenging if not almost impossible to monitor, measure or manage. Take, for example:

Sales Performance =
Ability x Motivation x Environment

Or:

Sales Performance =
Capacity (Competencies x Resources x Opportunity) x Commitment

Based on experience, the one that works best is:

Sales Performance = Readiness x Productivity x Efficiency x Effectiveness

It captures all of the primary factors that actually do drive sales performance, and which include:

1 **Marketing capability** – Readiness
2 **Superior people** – Readiness, Productivity, Efficiency, Effectiveness
3 **Robust rewards, incentive schemes and structure** – Productivity, Effectiveness
4 **Metrics** – Efficiency, Productivity
5 **Pipeline management process** – Effectiveness
6 **Account management process** – Effectiveness
7 **Systems** – Productivity, Efficiency
8 **Sales management and leadership team** – Readiness, Effectiveness

1. MARKETING CAPABILITY

It goes without saying that you are not going to sell much if you do not have the right product, or one that is not priced correctly or has no visibility in the market. A company might have the best sales team, but if the totality of the proposition including the experience is weak, then that business can forget about sales. It really is essential to have a superior marketing capability in place as well, when trying to develop a company's sales performance.

2. SUPERIOR PEOPLE

As in any business function, getting the right people on board is job number one. Hiring sales folks is more a black art than a skill, and calls for an appreciation that there are peculiar personality traits that are imperatives to succeed in sales (as the table shows).

1 **Self confidence:** Look for people who believe that they can achieve anything.

2 **Ambition:** Look for audacious, ambitious people who are often very competitive and do not like to lose.

3 **People friendly:** This is obvious. Anyone who is uncomfortable with strangers is definitely not cut for sales.

4 **Empathy:** Look for people who can connect and relate with their potential customers.

5 **Tough mindedness:** Look out for folks who can accept rejection (and often humiliation) from potential customers.

6 **Composure:** A seemingly calm, cool, composed and collected sales person exudes confidence.

7 **Control:** Sales professionals need to be self disciplined to achieve. They need to exercise self control to manage and reach their targets.

8 **Endurance:** The ability to endure long, tedious and often unpleasant negotiations internally and externally is a critical requirement for any good sales person.

9 **Sense of urgency:** Despite their calm exterior, a good sales professional needs have a sense of urgency – as if there is no tomorrow. This is often exhibited by good sales professionals as they do not want to take chances with any opportunity.

10. **Individualistic:** Good sales professionals are primarily motivated by the rewards and nothing else.

3. ROBUST REWARDS, INCENTIVE SCHEMES AND STRUCTURE

Sustaining a high-performance sales team requires a robust, dynamic and attractive reward and incentive structure. Without it, the sales performance will not be sustainable. We need to understand that the primary motivator for excellent sales professionals is money. This may sound crude and against conventional wisdom, which purports that there are other motivators beyond money. It could be so in other functions, but definitely not for the top sales performers. Applying the 80:20 rule requires that top performers are rewarded well. If 70 to 80% of sales come from 20 to 30% of the sales team, then it is important that the top sales performers are rewarded beyond the traditional incentive structure.

4. METRICS

An essential requirement for any successful sales organization is to have appropriate metrics that are fair, simple and measurable and ones which add to the bottom line of the business. Some common metrics include a combination of customer acquisition, retention, up-selling, cross-selling and collection dimensions. The metrics should also include efficiency factors like number of customer visits, lead times, new accounts added and others. Remember, what cannot be measured cannot be managed and if it cannot be managed then we have utterly failed in our responsibility as business leaders.

5. PIPELINE MANAGEMENT PROCESS

Managing the sales pipeline a.k.a. the sales funnel is an essential requirement to building a world-class sales organization. Many good sales professionals use a Qualify, Propose, Negotiate, Close process to ensure they are focusing on the right thing with each customer prospect at the right time.

Most B2B sales engagement goes through a classic cycle. First targets are identified from the prospect list, contacts are established, needs are assessed and a proposal is given to a potential customer. Then negotiations occur before a sale is concluded as a firm order. The trick to managing a sales operation is knowing reliably the number of customers, and the potential deal size in each stage of the sales cycle. This needs be a robust process, which does not allow sales folks to arbitrarily assign probabilities at each stage of the sales cycle.

For example, if no contact has been established with a key decision-maker or key influencer in a target organization, assigning any probability beyond zero percent is foolhardy and will only falsely inflate the size and value of the sales pipeline. Assigning predetermined and correct probabilities to the sales process will help in identifying risks, and in achieving the desired sales targets.

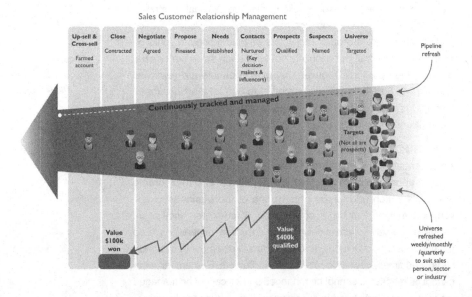

Figure 11: To achieve your desired sales target, each stage of the pipeline must be tightly managed.

Based on the market sector and experience, a sales professional having a quarterly target of say $400,000 will need at least 4x of their stated target in the 'contact established' stage of the sales pipeline to meet the quarter end target goal.

Knowing the deal value of the pipeline of their team at any time is an essential responsibility for any sales manager. But that is only part of it. A critical aspect of pipeline management is to ensure that the sales team is dealing with companies that have the budget (B), that the person(s) they are dealing with have the authority (A) and there is a real need (N). Assigning a predetermined BAN score to pipeline management will ensure its validity.

Having a robust pipeline management framework is critical to identifying and knowing if the sales team is functioning to full capacity – and if the business is really going to make it or not.

It is too important a task to be left to others, and calls for regular and structured discussions with the sales management team to confirm the constant accuracy of the pipeline. The pipeline should be a shared across other business functions including marketing, finance and manufacturing, so there are no surprises at month end.

6. ACCOUNT MANAGEMENT PROCESS

A structured account management process has two primary components of account planning and the account review process:

Account planning process: Every good sales professional will have a structured account plan for all major accounts. The account plan should articulate the prospect's business, its compelling rationale to consider the proposition on offer, its end-user needs and others. Sales professionals should know the nature of any compelling event that might trigger a sales opportunity (like M&A, right-sizing, cost reduction efforts, growth or lack of it, etc). The account plan will also clearly identify the opportunity size, possibilities for all products, and key competitor strengths and weaknesses review. Other pertinent factors in an account plan should clearly identify all the key decision-makers and influencers and the plans to engage with each of them. Knowing the account well will help any sales professional offer a compelling value proposition to each and every potential customer.

Account review process: There needs to be review process at all levels of the hierarchy of the company. Of course the number of accounts that are reviewed at the highest levels will only be limited to the largest opportunities. Every sales manager, sales director or higher will need to conduct a review of the opportunities of their team, to identify potential weaknesses and identify areas where they could better support the sales folks. The account review of the largest opportunities needs be cross-functional, as it should intend to get all the functions in the company engaged to achieve a win for the sales team. A cross-functional account review of the largest opportunities will also help identify risks and inconsistencies in the pipeline.

7. SYSTEMS

The sales team is hired to sell, and should not be overloaded with bureaucratic paperwork and back-office duties. Any sales team that spends less than 75% of its time out selling, meeting customers and new prospects is not doing what it is supposed to. Automated sales support systems should be put in place, or cheap clerical support hired to carry out the back-office sales administration functions. There is a high opportunity cost for any business that uses its sales teams to do back-office work. To maintain the integrity of the sales pipeline, it is worthwhile investing in systems to automate opportunity management of the sales pipeline. There are many affordable pay per user monthly solutions available in the market.

EVEN WITH A FANTASTIC SALES TEAM, HAVING A BAD MANAGER CAN DE-MOTIVATE THE TOP PERFORMERS, resulting in the risk of them leaving the company. It is essential therefore, to pay special attention to the person hired to lead this very critical and important function.

8. SALES MANAGEMENT AND LEADERSHIP TEAMS

It is often misunderstood that a good sales manager has to be good sales professional. A good sales person often does not necessarily make a good sales manager. A good manager might make a good sales person. Beyond the traditional competencies required of a manager, the art of managing a sales team requires that the person leading the sales team must be inspiring, motivating and fair. The sales management team's primary goal is to ensure that there are no risks to achieving the sales targets. It is the sales manager's responsibility to ensure that the team is able to and can deliver the targets given to it. He or she will often be expected to be a fair arbiter of conflicts within their teams.

NOTES

EVERY SALE IS A BATTLE WON FOR THE COMPANY. MARKETING IS ABOUT WINNING THE WAR IN THE MARKETPLACE, WHICH CANNOT BE WON WITHOUT THE SUCCESS OF INDIVIDUAL BATTLES.

SALES AND MARKETING, BATTLES AND WARS

The differences between the two key functions and why you need to allocate resources for both

I n most organizations the functional activities of marketing and sales are misunderstood, and in small businesses they are often actually combined into a single function. In both scenarios it is important to understand the differences of each function, to ensure that adequate resources are put in place to cover every aspect of these critical operations.

There can be recurring catfights and disagreements between the marketing and the sales functions in most organizations. Some of the sources of disagreements are valid, some are dubious and others plain stupid. Some of the perceptions about sales and about marketing are correct and are often perpetuated by actions from both sides. One common perception among the sales folks is that "marketing is out of touch with reality" whilst the marketers often contend that "sales are not selling well enough, and are myopic in their approach to the market". These sorts of perception are sometimes true, and often occur due to a lack of understanding of the importance that each role plays (and should play) for their mutual successes.

There definitely exists a cultural and knowledge gap between these two most critical functions in a company – and neither can succeed without the other.

Sell = Selling, Market = Marketing

Try asking potential candidates applying for a marketing job to describe in their own words their understanding of the differences between marketing and sales. It will generate some interesting views and many misconceptions about the functions. There is never a right or wrong answer to the question, of course, but some opinions do make more sense than others.

Some that don't show any great insight on the part of candidates are those that insist "marketing is all about PR", "marketing does brand", or that "marketing does ads". In the same vein, "sales does push and marketing does pull". An all time favorite must be that "sales work for commission and marketing does not get commission". Whilst all these answers may be partially true, the differences between sales and marketing are much more significant than these uninformed quotes might infer.

As a marketer, let me first pay tribute to all the sales folks who slog day in and day out often under extreme conditions of weather, risk to income, personal humility, safety and others.

Wikipedia defines sales as the pinnacle activity involved in the selling of products or services in return for money or other compensation. It is an act of completion of a commercial activity. It certainly is the pinnacle activity in that sales have to overcome the cognitive dissonance of all buyers at the moment when cash is dished out, or when an order for goods and services are issued.

American author, salesman, and motivational speaker Zig Ziglar has said that every sale has five basic obstacles:

- **no need,**

- **no money,**

- **no hurry,**

- **no desire,**

- **no trust.**

So to overcome these obstacles and to meet their business targets, the sales folks have to be liked, trusted and known! Sales have to succeed each and every time. With tough targets and extreme market conditions, the good folks in sales cannot afford to have an 'off day,' particularly because most sales jobs have a high variable component in their compensation package. It can mean the difference between a salesman having a job or not, or being able to pay the monthly rental, mortgage or car loan installments! So we need to salute the constant capability that is displayed by sales.

As for marketing, it is all about winning in the marketplace. There have been many definitions written about what marketing is and two in particular, when read together, make perfect sense. Drucker defines it as "Marketing is not only much broader than selling, it is not a specialized activity at all. It encompasses the entire business. It is the whole business seen from the point of view of the final result, that is, from the customer's point of view". Palmer defines it as "Marketing is essentially about marshalling the resources of an organization so that they meet the changing needs of the customer on whom the organization depends."

In many ways marketing is responsible for delivering growth. Without growth, no company will sustain. So how does marketing do that?

- **Marketing has to anticipate**, understand the business and to be able to deliver the customer needs. In order to do this, marketing has to be to be plugged into know, understand and act on the changes and trends in the industry and technology.

- **Marketing has to have deep insights** on the customer needs. This means that marketing will have to ensure that the physical, logical, visual (and other sensory) and emotional experience of the customer is encompassed in the totality of the proposition.

- **Marketing** – as the owner of the customer value proposition – **has to delight their customers** with differentiated and superior products that are priced correctly (optimally), and communicated so that the marketers' brand and services are market aware, functional and relevant for its users.

- **Marketing has to create a totality** of customer experience (physical, sensory, emotional, logical etc) that augurs loyalty and emotional bonding to the brand. In addition, the marketer will have to determine optimally viable go-to-market strategies and tactics that ensure optimal channel economics, reach, coverage, access and others.

And does marketing do it all alone? Of course not! Marketing will have to orchestrate across the various business and operational functions that deliver the different aspects of the proposition. Whilst all these functions are important, the success of the sales teams (across all channels) in getting the customer to pay for a company's products or services will be the pinnacle of the commercial activity that will ultimately determine if a marketer's effort is fruitful.

So what then is the difference between marketing and sales?

One way to look at it is that every sales interaction is an individual battle. Every sale is a battle won for the company. Marketing is about winning the war in the marketplace, which cannot be won without the success of individual battles – and there is no point in winning a battle, if you cannot win the war!

NOTES

DIRECT MARKETING IS ALL ABOUT THE MARKETING COMMUNICATIONS OF A 'FOR PROFIT' COMPANY WHERE DIRECT CONTACT IS MADE… BETWEEN A SELLER OF PRODUCTS, PROPOSITIONS AND SERVICES AND ITS CURRENT AND POTENTIAL CUSTOMERS.

THE ART OF DIRECT MARKETING – WHY DIRECT MARKETING MATTERS

Clearing the confusion about this highly effective sales tool and defining its scope

D irect marketing is a highly effective sales tool that all businesses will want to deploy as part of their everyday marketing activity. Notably, it is one of the most cost-efficient ways smaller businesses can acquire new customers, retain existing customers and/or increase the revenue potential of an existing base of customers.

For all its relevance to business, direct marketing is one of those terms that has the potential to confuse. It is so, because most marketers feel that any marketing activity, promotion or communication will invoke a direct response from the customer. In fact, nothing could be further from the truth.

Direct marketing is all about the marketing communications of a 'for profit' company, where direct contact is made, initiated or invited between a seller of products, propositions and services, and its current and potential customers. It can involve direct mail, direct response advertising (including infomercials and teleshopping), personal selling and telemarketing.

Whatever the type, importantly the results of any direct marketing activity should be able to be directly measured, to assess the intended or the actual financial return on that investment. In other words, a marketer should be able to exploit the relationship that exists between a business and its prospects or customers as individuals. One way to better understand the fundamentals of direct marketing is to explore the key differences in mass advertising versus direct marketing:

Mass advertising	Direct marketing
Breadth of coverage	Depth of relationship building potential
Communicated to the masses	Communicated to a target audience
Wins attention of all, including competitors	Wins attention of a targeted selective universe of intended customers
Elicits recall or remembrance	Elicits a direct response
Generates a customer's functional or emotional impression	Leads to a customer making a decision
Campaigns are costed according to the whole universe of potential customers	Campaigns are costed according to the size of a targeted and segmented cluster of customers

Figure 12: The primary differences between mass advertising and direct marketing.

Before getting into the details of direct marketing tactics, it is important we fully understand the advantages and disadvantages of direct marketing.

Advantages

1 **Customer experience** Done well, direct marketing offers the capability for businesses to give customers a better experience than mass marketing.

2 **Deeper customer relationships** It offers the capability for businesses to build deep relationships and segregate their customers as individuals. Direct marketing also has the potential to build continuing relationship with an existing customer, especially where the business is able to maintain and manage a customer database that captures all relevant information on a customer (for comparison, try to imagine the information or rather the lack of it on 'walk in' customers in a traditional retail environment).

3 **Test marketing capability** Direct marketing enables the marketer to test markets and take measures as to what works and what does not work.

4 **Flexibility and predictability** Direct marketing enables marketers a good degree of flexibility to manage and control their costs, and comes with an ability to predict and measure the outcomes of a campaign.

5 **Higher customer motivation to respond** Direct marketing has a higher preponderance for customers to be motivated to respond.

6 **Enables customer segmentation** Direct marketing enables the marketer to better segment or cluster their customers.

Disadvantages

1 **Consequential loss** Wrongly or poorly executed direct marketing strategies can have tremendous negative consequences for a business.

2 **Reputational damage** Junk mail, annoying telemarketers and intrusive direct sales folks have given direct marketing tactics a bad image.

3 **Opportunity costs, through inaccurate targeting** Inaccurate and out-dated mailing lists can not only become a costly disaster but can increase the annoyance factor of potential customers.

4 **Lack of emotional stimuli** By its very nature, direct marketing is too direct for many customer prospects, and does not have the potential to create the stimuli to invoke an emotional response from a potential buyer.

When do you use direct marketing

Direct marketing is most effectively used when:

- There is a narrowly defined target.
- There is a need to explain the proposition in detail.
- There is a need to elicit a direct response from a potential or existing customer.

It is most effective when two critical success factors are fully considered before embarking or executing the campaign:

- **Target selection:** professional marketers fully understand that it is paramount that when they select a target, it has to be based on the potential interest or pre-existing levels of interest of a selected target.

- **Proposition strength:** a strong campaign needs to market a strong proposition that will provoke or elicit a strong response.

It is important here also to recognize some of the received wisdoms of the direct marketer:

1 **The more we need potential customers to react,** the less willing they appear to be.

2 **The more the level of resistance** from a potential and existing customer base, the more expensive it will be to buy the cost of sales time (i.e. the direct marketing costs).

3 **There is an inverse proportionality** to the cost of persuasion and a pre-existing interest within a pool of potential targets. What this means is that it will cost a lot of money to persuade a customer to bite the bait if they are unaware of a proposition or lack any interest in it, or if the direct marketing list is not targeted correctly.

4 **The life-time value of the customer matters greatly.** There is a direct relationship to the life-time value of the customer and the acquisition costs: the life-time value of a customer decreases, the more it costs to acquire that customer.

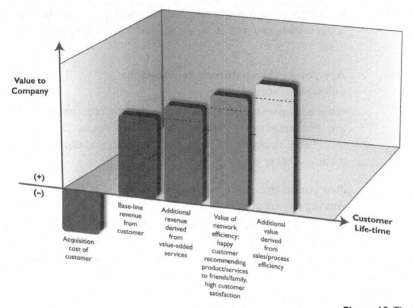

Figure 13: The life-time value of retaining customers.

Managing the customer life-time value

In view of the impact that the life-time value of a customer can have on the return-on-investment of direct marketing campaigns, we need to consider how best we can build a life-time relationship with our customers.

Customer Relationship Management (CRM) has been a buzzword that has been around for a good while. It has mostly been described in the context of IT systems, business processes, opportunity management and so forth. However, marketers will prefer to consider CRM from a direct marketing perspective, and there are three phases that need be outlined, all of which will shape the nature and execution of a direct marketing campaign.

Are you in the customer relationship formation stage?

This phase is used to reinforce a potential customers' decision to purchase. As a marketer we need to be certain that we have an offer which has benefits that interest the customer.

Reinforcement of a customers' decision could include the fulfillment and/or delivery aspects of the proposition that the business is trying to sell.

Are you in the customer relationship cultivation stage?

We should ask if we are able to personalize the relationship in some way that better meets the customers' unique needs. The marketer should also consider if the business is attempting to build trust and/or if it able to better qualify the customer.

Are you in the customer relationship management stage?

At this stage, we need to consider if the business is able to provide a value proposition to meet the customers' unique needs. If so, it has a greater potential to cross-sell and up-sell the existing propositions.

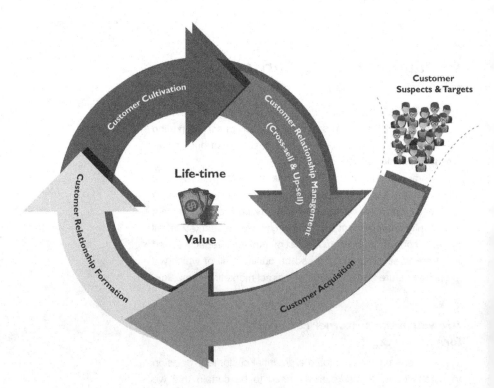

Figure 14: The value economics of direct marketing.

NOTES

DIRECT MARKETING GIVES CUSTOMERS THE TOTALITY OF EXPERIENCE *THAT NO OTHER MARKETING TOOL CAN PROVIDE, AND WHICH INCLUDES THE ELEMENTS OF SIGHT, SOUND AND TOUCH AS WELL AS LOGICAL EXPERIENCE.*

HOW TO IDENTIFY, CHOOSE AND APPLY THE RIGHT DIRECT MARKETING TACTICS

Tactics to sharpen the execution of direct marketing activities

Now that we understand some of the advantages and disadvantages of direct marketing, its key success factors and when to use direct marketing, and how to manage the relationship with the customer, it is time to discuss each of the main direct marketing tactics in detail.

Direct mail

The following tactics for direct mail can be considered as recommended practise for managing a campaign:

- **Make sure** that the visual and logical experience is superb, 'eye catching' and truly different (remember we have only four seconds to involve and engage the customer!).

- **That the targets are well defined** and pre-selected based on the business' objectives.

- **Make sure that the value proposition** differs significantly from that of the competition (keep in mind the obvious – do not alert your competition of your direct mail campaign/s).

- **Consider factors such as the size** and differentiation of the envelope, the day of the week when the direct mail is mailed out, the reliability of the postal system and the uniqueness of the direct mail design.

From experience, it is not to be recommended to try and save money by insisting on low quality post cards or by minimizing the size of the direct mail shot.

THERE IS LITTLE POINT IN ENGAGING WITH A DIRECT MAIL CAMPAIGN, if it does not differentiate itself from the millions of junk mail items delivered to consumers each year.

Direct response advertising

The tactics for direct response advertising should also always include a 'call to action' which should always be vivid, direct and conspicuous!

- **Consider direct marketing tactics**, modes and methods such as magazines that include bind-in insert cards, toll free numbers in newspapers and magazines, infomercials and teleshopping channels. These allow us as marketers to emphasize the prime benefit and the total proposition wrap.

- **Tricky, complicated openings rarely work**. It helps if the brand name is well known, and if it is, ensure that it is featured conspicuously in the collateral.

- **Make coupons into mini-ads,** complete with the business, the brand name, the promise, and a miniature image of the proposition itself.

As a special note on direct response advertising, the prevalence of campaigns in developed markets like the US, Europe and Japan, now mean the attitudes of potential buyers are ambivalent at best. However, in the emerging and growth markets such as the Middle East, South Asia and South East Asia and Africa, this direct marketing tactic has a huge potential to drive customers to the business.

Personal selling or direct sales

Personal selling is the end-to-end process of face-to-face communications with existing or potential target customers and all of the persuasion activities this involves. For any business, deploying a direct sales team is most effective:

- When the propositions or services are/have relatively higher total cost of ownership and/or are higher priced.
- When the propositions or services are complex or complicated in nature.
- When the propositions or services are tailored/customized to the customers' needs
- When the propositions or services offer opportunities to cross-sell or up-sell, or if they provide opportunities for the customer to trade in.
- When the decision process about the propositions or services is complex and/or when decisions are made at the point of purchase.

There are several factors that come into play before deciding if a direct sales team is the best option for a direct marketing campaign:

- **Order taking** – is the direct sales effort just an order taking tactic? If so, change it now.
- **Technology consulting** – is the business dependent on the direct sales force to enable and empower the customer to have more technical information, advice, and service?
- **Complex propositions** – are the propositions sophisticated and complex?
- **System selling** – is the proposition an end-to-end system of propositions, products or services?

- **Continuous improvement mission** – is the sales team on a mission of purpose, calling on accounts for purposes of monitoring the satisfaction of buyers and updating the buyers' needs?

From experience, in emerging and developing markets the channel and marketing economics make direct sales an effective direct marketing tool for smaller businesses. Direct sales marketing campaigns are one of the most effective ways in which a business can promote a proposition:

- **It gives customers the totality of experience** that no other marketing tool can provide, and which includes the elements of sight, sound, and touch as well as logical experience (a proposition sometimes will enable taste / smell as well, in some sectors!).

- **It enables pre-selection** and an ability to demonstrate the benefits of a proposition much better that any other means.

- **It provides focus**, because once the attention of a customer or a potential target has been won, there is no other competition to enable their cognitive dissonance.

ON THE DOWNSIDE TELEMARKETING IS VERY EXPENSIVE on a cost-per-contact basis, and a major portion of customer prospects are not reachable. Telemarketing campaigns can also prove to be annoying to customers, they do not have the flexibility of direct mail, and the delivery option is fixed.

Telemarketing

Telemarketing is rightly considered one of the most potent direct marketing tools for several reasons:

- **Potential and existing customers** can be selectively targeted.

- **Success and impact** of a campaign can be monitored and tracked.

- **Different scripts and delivery formats** can be used and experimentation is simple and practical.

- **Provides a live and constructive dialogue** with the customer.

- **Offers a customer almost a totality of experiences,** including sound, logic and a chemistry.

Hitting the target with well measured effectiveness of direct marketing

Direct marketing is an expensive tactic to implement and therefore selecting the right target is vitally important. Some key considerations include crucial B2C direct marketing demographics, such as:

- Age
- Income
- Gender
- Marital status
- Nationality / Creed
- Homeowner
- Dwelling type (home or apartment)
- Mail order buying habits (by product type)
- Interests
- Married or divorced or single?
- Presence and number of children
- Geography

Figure 15:
Understanding and evaluating the CPI and CPO is critical to the successful execution of a direct marketing strategy.

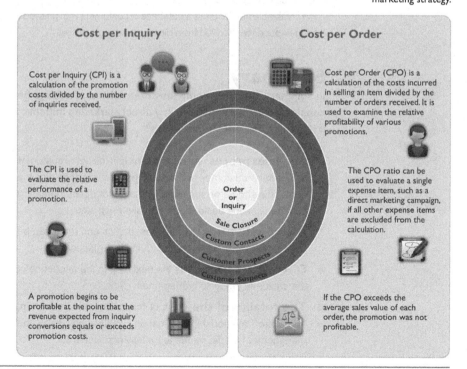

Cost per Inquiry

Cost per Inquiry (CPI) is a calculation of the promotion costs divided by the number of inquiries received.

The CPI is used to evaluate the relative performance of a promotion.

A promotion begins to be profitable at the point that the revenue expected from inquiry conversions equals or exceeds promotion costs.

Cost per Order

Cost per Order (CPO) is a calculation of the costs incurred in selling an item divided by the number of orders received. It is used to examine the relative profitability of various promotions.

The CPO ratio can be used to evaluate a single expense item, such as a direct marketing campaign, if all other expense items are excluded from the calculation.

If the CPO exceeds the average sales value of each order, the promotion was not profitable.

Order or Inquiry

Sale Closure

Custom Contacts

Customer Prospects

Customer Suspects

Other B2B direct marketing demographics that may need to be considered include:

- Vertical or industry market
- Number of employees
- Revenue
- Title and responsibility of the person to whom the direct marketing campaign is addressed to
- Information on all influencers and decision makers
- The credit worthiness of the organization
- Geography
- Number of branches, sites and/or offices
- Number of laptops or desktops
- Fixed assets versus employee size

Experienced direct marketers often use a simple RFM model which is based on the propensity for a customer to respond and buy from or through a direct marketing campaign. The model works on the premise that if a customer has purchased Recently, Frequently and if the size of the Monetary value of the purchase is relatively high, then there is a higher preponderance for that existing customer to buy again.

An invaluable asset here is a database of customers with previous buying experience, derived from direct marketing activities.

Summary

In summary, there are some unwritten rules that need to be considered before deploying any direct marketing initiative, if it is to be considered a success:

- **The sales process and sequence** is the set of customer or potential customer decision steps necessary to close a deal. This should be matched with a set of direct marketing communications designed to provoke each step.
- **Direct marketing strategies**, tactics and tools can be used to narrow the universe to 'qualified prospects'.
- **Direct marketing sells** the next step in the sequence of the customer lifecycle management cycle.
- **The totality of the cost** of the customer relationship, from the relationship formation, cultivation and the management stage, needs to be fully accounted for.

NOTES

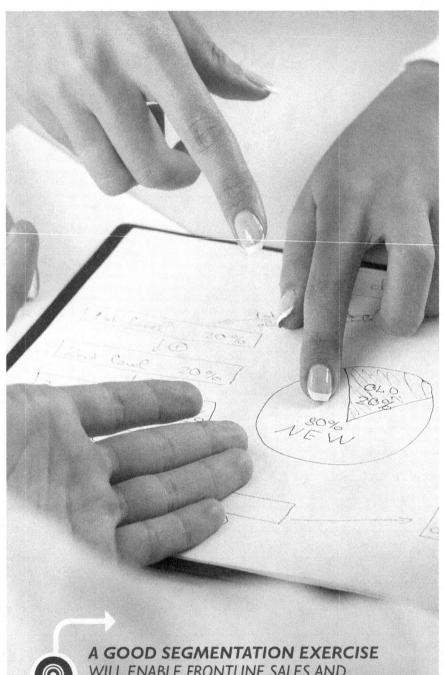

A GOOD SEGMENTATION EXERCISE WILL ENABLE FRONTLINE SALES AND SERVICE FOLKS IDENTIFY CUSTOMERS ACCORDING TO THE CUSTOMER SEGMENT HE OR SHE BELONGS TO.

NOT ALL CUSTOMERS ARE CREATED EQUAL – THE ART OF SEGMENTATION

The essence of a market and how you can make sure your customers are ready, willing and able

One of the unwritten secrets of successful business is that not all customers should be treated equal! But marketers normally execute the application of their segmentation strategies too narrowly. It is short-sighted to look at segmentation in a single dimension, clustering customers in homogenous groups for marketing purposes only. This is a fallacy as segmentation drives the very essence of how an organization operates, serves and meets the needs of all of its customers in the market. There is a tendency too, to think only in generic terms about what it is that makes a market, and before marketing a proposition to a customer segment it is important to think through the essence of what a market is:

1 **A market has to have customers** with unmet needs or wants. If there is no unmet need, or if the value proposition does not offer any incremental improvement over market norms, or if the proposition isn't differentiated, then there is no point in being in business.

2 **Consumers and/or business customers** should have a proven willingness to buy. "Build it and they will come" is for the brave and the foolish.

3 **There has to be buying power.** Consumers and business customers have to able to afford what is on offer.

4 **Last not least,** whoever is being targeted as the customer has to have the authority to buy.

In other words, how do you make sure that your customers are ready, willing and able? It is vital this simple logic is held front of mind, before embarking on any expensive proposition development or customer segmentation exercise.

Figure 16: For segmentation to be practical, it must meet four fundamental criteria.

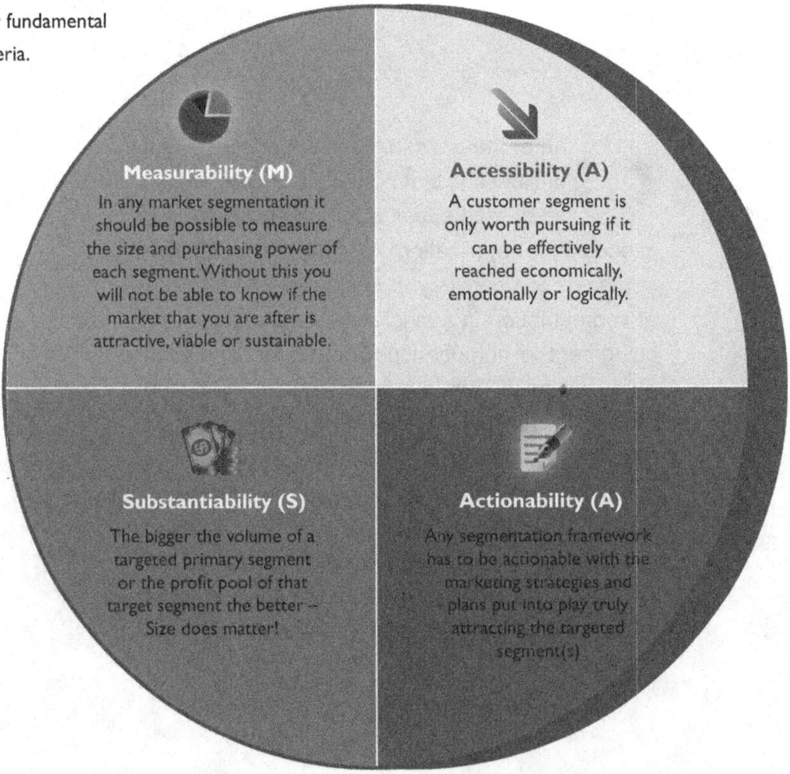

Measurability (M)
In any market segmentation it should be possible to measure the size and purchasing power of each segment. Without this you will not be able to know if the market that you are after is attractive, viable or sustainable.

Accessibility (A)
A customer segment is only worth pursuing if it can be effectively reached economically, emotionally or logically.

Substantiability (S)
The bigger the volume of a targeted primary segment or the profit pool of that target segment the better – Size does matter!

Actionability (A)
Any segmentation framework has to be actionable with the marketing strategies and plans put into play truly attracting the targeted segment(s)

Market segmentation work-out – MASA in practise

Segmentation is commonly known as a process in which customers are grouped or clustered into homogenous groups based on demographics, psychographics, needs, spending patterns, cultural background, education, language, mobility and others. Segmentation is not just for marketing purposes. A segmentation strategy will help target and attract customers better, but will also help set the tone and a framework on how to serve customers, and how to organize to serve customers better.

Most folks often ignore the fundamental rules of segmentation – those that get it right, clearly understand and follow the MASA rules...

1 **Market segmentation is often done** through a combination of primary and secondary research. There are many approaches and a common way is to first carry out a set of qualitative studies (using focus groups of a limited size and number). The outcome of these qualitative studies is then used to formulate a segmentation hypothesis, which can be validated through a detailed primary research program, encompassing a much larger and statistically valid sample. The segments or clusters can then be derived using statistics and modeling.

2 **The outcome of a good segmentation exercise** will not only allow the size and value of each segment to be accurately grouped, but should also enable you to develop portraits of each customer segment. The portrait of a customer segment could include their lifestyle and values, priorities, aspirations, needs, demographics, attitudes and preferences to your company's and competitors' products and services.

3 **A good market segmentation framework** will help to design and craft a proposition that is relevant to a target segment. It will also help shape retention strategies that prevent customer churn and business losses in certain segments, well as steering more effective communications spending.

OTHER VALUABLE INFORMATION COULD INCLUDE triggers and barriers to adoption, and how disposable income is spent as well as internet, TV viewing and print readership habits, among many others.

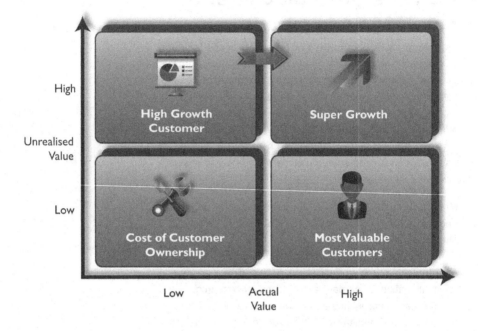

High

Unrealised Value

Low

High Growth Customer

Super Growth

Cost of Customer Ownership

Most Valuable Customers

Low   Actual Value   High

Figure 17: The cost-to-serve analysis is essential for the growth of your business.

4 **With segmentation comes an opportunity** to develop optimal and differentiated pricing strategies for different segments. After all, when economists refer to a demand curve, they are actually referring to the aggregate average demand curve across all different segments in the market. (Now we can see the link between marketing and macroeconomics!)

5 **A good segmentation exercise** will also enable frontline sales and service folks identify customers according to the customer segment he or she belongs to. (Just imagine the opportunity costs lost in trying to close a deal with a wrong prospect!)

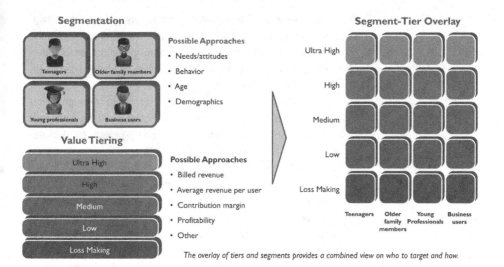

Figure 18: An overlay of value-based segmentation can be used to ensure high value customers are identified for royal treatment.

Two-dimensional value-based segmentation models – Customer value matters

The ultimate goal for business is to turn a profit. The trick then is to find ways of increasing the level of product profitability, customer by customer, year on year.

Businesses generally have a good handle on their manufacturing costs, their distribution costs or their point of sale costs – expressed as a percentage of revenue, or in terms of unit cost per item. What is often less well understood in business are the total costs relating to a particular customer and the so-called cost-to-serve.

Cost-to-serve involves analysis and quantification of all the activities and costs incurred to fulfill customer demand for a product through the entire supply chain. It's a well-established approach for exploring which customers and products matter most to company profitability, and how to manage them at the appropriate cost.

Cost-to-serve is fundamental to profitability and understanding its influence on the bottom line is vital. It needs to be closely watched because without cost-to-serve indicators across the different customer segments, a business can't even begin to improve product profitability.

Market-based segmentation alone is never enough. The economics of customer experience dictate that the intended experience should be designed based on the profitability derived from a value-based segment. When 20% of your customers can generate about 80% of revenues, then resources have to be disproportionately allocated to the ones that matter.

Value-based segmentation will help ensure that customer services are prioritised at all customer touch points, and it will ensure that credit and collections policies reflect the dependency of profits on high-value customers. A single dimension market-based segmentation alone is not enough. An overlay of a value-based segmentation can be used to ensure that high value customers are properly identified as deserving the royal treatment they are given!

NOTES

WE NEED TO CHECK THAT OUR VALUE PROPOSITIONS *GIVE OUR CUSTOMERS THE OPPORTUNITY TO SUCCUMB TO TEMPTATION AND COMMIT AS MANY OF THE CONSUMERIST SINS AS POSSIBLE!*

ENTICING AND TEMPTING YOUR CUSTOMERS TO SIN

The seven deadly consumerist sins and how they can add to your bottom line

W e've all heard of (and occasionally may have committed?) one or more of the seven deadly sins. These 'cardinal sins' or 'capital vices' have evolved over time and were translated from Ancient Greek into Latin and into almost every modern language there after. Mahatma Gandhi had his own list, his so-called Seven Blunders of the World that included Wealth without Work, Politics without Principle and Commerce without Morality. Today's marketer will want to play to the modern all-important Conspicuous Consumption version of the sins, which are:

1. **Extravagance and greed**
2. **Gluttony**
3. **Pride**
4. **Lust**
5. **Wrath**
6. **Sloth**
7. **Envy**

Extravagance is the luxury of the poor, penury is the luxury of the rich" *Oscar Wilde*

It's worth keeping these seven deadly sins in mind, as you develop the value proposition for your customers – because almost all of them will succumb to one or more of them! We need to be mindful of human frailties and the temptations affecting our customers! And we need to check that our value propositions give our customers the opportunity to succumb to temptation and commit as many of these consumerist sins as possible!

Extravagance and greed are unrestrained excess. Marketers in every industry will pay heed to entice their customers to be extravagant. In whatever business you are in, it always pays to entice your customers to spend more, to buy that extra something that they will not fully use, or to treat a loved one to a special gift or extravagance. Check and recheck if your value propositions offer customers the opportunity to be extravagant and that it is worth it. Ensure the value proposition allows customers to be extravagant – so they can buy something they don't necessarily need immediately, buy more than what they need, or pay more than what they intended, and so on.

> **Three great forces rule the world: stupidity, fear and greed"**
>
> *Albert Einstein*

Extravagance and greed are often thought to apply to excessive or rapacious desire and pursuit of wealth, status and power. But how many of us have had an exclusive invitation from a credit card company, an airline or other service providers that seem to imply that we have a special status? Marketers of luxury goods thrive on bringing out the greed in all of us! Do we really need that $5,000 handbag? It is the divine duty of all marketers to poach customers away from alternative propositions sold by the competition; therefore, betrayal for personal gain can also be considered greed.

As greed and extravagance are inordinate desires to acquire or possess more than what is needed or deserved, especially with respect to material wealth, this is an easy one for marketers. Communicating subtle or direct aspirational messages helps bring out the greed trait in all of us. So the next time you see that credit card company message or the designer goods ad or the cell phone manufacturer's message touting for you to be cool with something new which you already have, remember, they are all playing to your sense of greed and extravagance!

If you are in the food services or hospitality industries, this is an easy sin to tempt your customers with! We all know gluttons, but they do not necessarily have to be just over-indulging or over-consuming food to be gluttonous. You can consume anything to a point of waste to be a glutton. Do you really need that iPhone, when you already have a Blackberry? How often do you need both? Isn't it just a waste? Offering a fixed-price buffet lunch is surely tempting the glutton in all of us. How about the wonderful buckets of minutes that your telecom provider offers? How about the 2 for 1s that a local supermarket or department store tempts shoppers with?

Gluttony is not a secret vice"
Orson Welles

These are wonderful and great propositions from a marketer's or a salesman's point of view as the incremental or marginal cost to offer the next or nth unit is minimal for the provider. If the actual cost is truly marginal or the opportunity cost is too high not to offer it, it behooves the marketer or the sales team to design and craft a value proposition so that customers are tempted to be gluttonous.

Pride is considered the original and most serious of the seven deadly sins, and the source of the other six. It is identified as a desire to be more important or attractive than others, failing to acknowledge the good work of others, and excessive love of self. (So my dear fellow marketers and sales professionals, this is an easy one for us!)

We will all want to excel in making our customers feel inferior for using a competitors' service or product, and conversely we make them feel superior for using our own 'well designed, perfect fit' propositions. The trait of personal pride (and vanity) is exploited in almost all industries: it is the reason so many marketers name their services Platinum, Superior, Super, Exclusive, and so forth. Its power is well understood when it

It is a beggar's pride that he is not a thief"
Japanese proverb

> *"Lust's passion will be served; it demands, it militates, it tyrannizes"*
> *Marquis De Sade*

comes to marketing or selling banking services, designer apparel or accessories. However, tempting customers with propositions that bring into play their dominant 'proud genes' is a ploy to be used in the hospitality industry and restaurants, in consulting businesses, politics, entertainment and almost every other sector.

Is any sin easier to sell than lust? Just think of it, almost all marketers seem to be selling lust. Some industries and companies take it to an extreme. Just take a moment and look at the airlines industry (in some countries), the entertainment and fashion industries, and the hospitality and restaurant sectors.

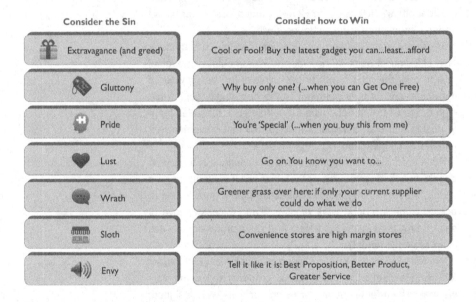

Consider the Sin	Consider how to Win
Extravagance (and greed)	Cool or Fool? Buy the latest gadget you can...least...afford
Gluttony	Why buy only one? (...when you can Get One Free)
Pride	You're 'Special' (...when you buy this from me)
Lust	Go on. You know you want to...
Wrath	Greener grass over here: if only your current supplier could do what we do
Sloth	Convenience stores are high margin stores
Envy	Tell it like it is: Best Proposition, Better Product, Greater Service

Figure 19: The golden rules of how you can win by tempting your customers to sin.

The US restaurant chain of Hooters is a good example: the trade name being taken from US slang for breasts, and its waiting staff made up mostly of young, attractive girls. These folks seem to have mastered the art of marketing and selling lust more than others.

Do they take time out occasionally to think about what their true intentions are, or to consider the impact of the models or spokespersons they select for their communications have on their customers? Even the ordinary testimonials from the supposedly ordinary people in their adverts appear to be extra ordinary.

Wrath, also known as anger or rage, may be described as inordinate and uncontrolled feelings of hatred. In its purest form, it may provoke antagonistic feelings towards someone, as hate.

This is one of the seven sins that I am personally very comfortable in tempting customers to commit. Imagine if we could get our customers' wrath on to our competitors. How could we do that, do I hear you ask? By making the customer realize that we have a better deal, that we offer a better customer experience and that considering other alternatives would not be a valid choice for them. Marketers and sales folks should repeatedly remind their customers what it is we are offering, and routinely remind them of what our competitor is not offering or is unable to do. This is called differentiating yourself in the market. Make the customer feel mad that his or her existing service provider or seller is not doing what your company is able to do.

Conversely, remember that it is good business sense not to irk your customers' wrath on to yourselves.

And wrath has left its scar – that fire of hell"
William Cullen Bryant

Sloth is considered more a sin of omission rather than commission. We all have been lazy one time or other. In this digital, 24 x 7 Internet age, we have a tremendous opportunity to make our customers lazy.

This is one other sin we should be happy to tempt our customers with. Taking away customer difficulties and offering conveniences which customers appreciate, makes for good commerce. Saving customers' time and money by tempting them with conveniences makes good sense for the customer and for your business. Any convenience that takes away

We excuse our sloth under the pretext of difficulty"
Marcus Fabius Quintillan

"Envy aims very high" *Ovid*

customer difficulties makes obvious sense. It also makes good business sense for us marketers and sales folks as it can often mean more sales, less costs and more profits.

Those who commit the sin of envy resent that another person has something they perceive themselves as lacking, and wish the other person to be deprived of it.

So what does this mean for marketing and sales? Well, get your competitors' customers to feel envious of your customers. Let them join you in droves after realizing the competitor was offering a poor deal, poor service or a faulty proposition. Invest marketing bucks in programs that make prospective customers aware of what they are missing – or what they must have to be like their fellow beings. Let prospects know that they don't need to be envious because the best proposition, better product or service is available to them easily, affordably and conveniently – through you.

But beware. Do not let your existing customers who have committed long term to you feel envious of your competitors' customers. Consider the customer who's committed to a 60-month car lease or someone who has signed a service contract with penalty provisions for early cancellation. Make them regret this and it is not only envy that you will elicit from the customer. You will also bear his or her full wrath. Hell hath no fury like a customer scorned!

Sinning all the way to seventh heaven?

So entice and expurgate, otherwise you will be effaced... be ebullient and enthused about getting more business and elating your customers, and always keep in mind the seven deadly consumerist sins.

Thou shall thus entice, espouse, exhort, elucidate, enlighten, and enthrall *your customers with your* effulgent *propositions keeping the seven deadly sins in your mind. Remember to expurgate the negative aspects of your proposition. If not, your competitor might efface you!*

Conspicuous Consumption Checkpoint

 1. Check and recheck if your value propositions offer customers the opportunity to be extravagant – and that it is worth it.

 2. Go big! When the incremental or marginal cost to offer the next or nth unit is marginal, the value proposition can be developed to have added appeal to the consumer glutton.

 3. The trait of personal pride (and vanity) is to be exploited with inclusive "VIP" marketing schemes.

 4. Consider how marketing messages and other customer communications stimulate the fourth consumerist sin of lust.

 5. Carry out an exercise to establish among customers and prospects how the brand differentiates itself from rival products and/or services to explore how this makes the customer cohorts feel. Which group is angry?

 6. Making it easy...save customers' time and money with sloth-inducing conveniences (such as online shopping baskets and self serve) and you will boost customer numbers and lower the cost of sale.

 7. Are your prospective customers aware of what they are missing – and are they being made to feel envious?

Figure 20: Tick off the items on this checklist and enable your customers to sin happily.

NOTES

DO NOT ASSUME THAT PAINTING A VENEER OF GLOSSY PINK ALL OVER THE MARKETING COLLATERAL IS ALL THAT IS INVOLVED IN MARKETING TO WOMEN. PINK IS NOT A BUSINESS STRATEGY!

WHY SHOULD SMES MARKET TO WOMEN?

Master the art of marketing to female buyers or your business will perish

Marketing to women needs to be included as a core part of business strategy of any company and there is an 'art of marketing to women' that is well worth exploring.

It could help shape an important growth tactic for business, and marketers can ill afford to ignore this most important of macro segments.

Do not assume that painting a veneer of glossy pink all over the marketing collateral is all that is involved in marketing to and targeting women. Pink is not a business strategy! Instead the very core of propositions and services need to be precision targeted to meet the unique needs of women.

Functional areas responsible for marketing, sales and overall business leadership are almost always overwhelmed by the male of the species. Yet men do not truly understand the unique needs and perspectives of women. Too many misdirected assumptions are made by men on how to woo women to their business. They need consider a famous quote from some unknown person (likely a woman, or a very wise man) – 'A woman can say more in a sigh than a man can say in a sermon.' Imagine that sigh reverberating across the world of social networks and you get the picture! Ignore your women customers at your peril!

Why marketing to women is relevant

Marketers will already be aware of some major global demographic, social, economic and technology shifts and marketing trends which are altering the traditional landscapes of businesses. Understanding these changes are essential to business survival and the sustainability of established business models.

DEMOGRAPHIC TRENDS

Women currently make up about 48% of the population in the world. So one in every two potential consumers or customers for a business, is a woman. In some age groups, globally women make up much more than half of the population. In the over 65 years age group, women make up about 56% of the population, explained by their longer life expectancy. Not only are older women healthier and more active in later life than men, but in many developed and developing economies, women over 50 have evolved from being a homemaker to being a purchaser of high ticket items. This should not be surprising and makes perfect sense, as once the children leave the nest these older but healthier and empowered women have a much higher disposable income.

IGNORING OR NOT REALLY UNDERSTANDING half of the potential customer base is definitely not a good business strategy. Yet look around any business of any size and it is abundantly clear how misrepresented in the work place women actually are.

SOCIO-ECONOMICS

All over the world, from Dubai to Dhaka to Dallas, the number of women entering the work force is increasing. What this means is that more women are of independent means and have more disposable incomes, and can spend more than ever before. It also means that women spend less time with their families. This has implications on how a business meets the needs of household goods and groceries sectors compared to items such as clothes, handbags, perfumes and the like that women buy or use for their personal use. One consequence is that marketers need to differentiate the experience when women shop during work days versus the weekends. Given their lack of time and hectic schedules balancing the demands of home and work, affordability, convenience and efficiency should almost always rule the design of any proposition, whether a woman is shopping for their household or for personal items. Given their busy schedules as care provider and career woman, it would be wise to note that women do appreciate having their 'own' time – which calls for marketers to design a different experience.

Globally, women now decide, influence or account for about at least 85% of all purchases. Most men (despite their personal experiences as a partner and/or husband), assume that this is only true of household and food items. This is certainly not the case. It includes large ticket items like houses, cars, selection of healthcare and financial services providers to white goods and others. In fact, women make the decisions or highly influence the purchase decision in almost anything ranging from vacations to purchase of technology items like PCs. This is not a truism for the developed economies alone. In any part of the world, women now exert a high influence on any purchase.

There are two other important and often ignored demographic trends that businesses need note. They are decreasing birth rates and increasing divorce rates both in developed and in developing economies. What this means is that women have more time for themselves and/or spend more time by themselves, have higher disposable income and are lesser influenced by a third party.

TECHNOLOGICAL SHIFTS:
WOMEN ARE DIGITAL SAVVY

Most women both in developed and developing economies are digitally savvy. They use the Internet for shopping, keep in touch with their friends through emails and instant messaging. They are very active in social networks like Facebook and Twitter. This has major implications for business marketers. The obvious one is that a large number of women shop online at least once a day. Given that women nurture and maintain relationships with friends better than men, they are more likely to pass on to their friends deals or savings that they have come across. Women are also more appreciative of a business's intent to serve them better. Therefore women are more like to respond positively to requests to serve on a select online product or service panel.

SO WOMEN NOT ONLY OFFER THE BEST CHANCE FOR REFERRALS, but they can better help a business improve its proposition to serve them better.

MARKETING TRENDS: CUSTOMER LOYALTY AND DETAIL ORIENTATION

Women focus on relationships better than men. Women see themselves as interdependent and more connected then men. Women will put in extra efforts to connect to people, society or even a business. Women focus on maintaining a relationship more than men. Women are more likely than men to give a business a second chance to serve them. Women do not show loyalty to an organization but rather to people in the organization.

This has huge implications for business owners and marketers who will want to ensure that they treat women as individuals and encourage one-on-one relationships. In this regard, SMEs do have a better chance of having close relationships with their women customers than larger organizations. They also have a better chance of promoting loyalty-based propositions to women, better than men.

Research has shown that women feel misunderstood in most marketing campaigns ranging from food, healthcare, automobiles and financial services. This represents a tremendous opportunity for businesses and marketers to garner insights and develop propositions which women understand and need. Women are more detail oriented than men. They look at the finer details of a sale, a deal or an offer. This is a double-edged sword for small business owners and SME marketers.

It is a known fact that women are more likely to use trade-in coupons promoting discounts than men are. They are also more likely to see if a proposition design is incomplete, or pick up the flaws in a proposition. Any business owner or marketer who ignores purposeful, structured and targeted marketing to women is making a costly mistake

A GOOD START WOULD BE TO HIRE MORE WOMEN and to ensure that the business strategy – and your personal leadership – fully takes into account the power of women.

NOTES

ENSURE THAT PRODUCT FEATURES ARE EASY TO USE, AND ARE ABLE TO DO WHAT WAS INTENDED. ADDING A DASH OF RELEVANT STYLE WILL DIFFERENTIATE IT AS A PROPOSITION TARGETED AT WOMEN.

RESPECTFUL MARKETING STRATEGIES AND TACTICS TARGETED AT WOMEN

Learn the key areas of difference and play to the desires and needs of the female market

Marketing in general requires a marketer to truly understand that a proposition takes in the end-to-end experience at all touch points across the customer lifecycle. Marketing to women also requires a proposition that takes into full account the differences, subtle or not, between men and women. There are a few differentiating factors and marketing engagement rules that will accentuate marketing efforts to women, and a few tips of marketing engagement that should be kept in mind.

1 **The design and form of the proposition should be easy to use, functional and stylish.** Although this would apply to any customer, it is really important to ensure that product features are easy to use, and are able to do what was intended. Adding a dash of relevant style will differentiate it as a proposition targeted at women.

2 **The brand credentials should be built with an established brand that already targets women as its primary customer base.** Aligning the proposition through a product bundling or channel alliance with established brands that have women as their primary targets, will help ensure that marketing gets the momentum it needs.

3 **Work with HR to include women as major part of the internal marketing and sales team.** Businesses need to ensure that women have a big role in their marketing and sales teams. This will not only ensure that the proposition design, function and style are commensurate to the needs of women, but will also ensure that communications efforts are not 'off message' and irrelevant.

4 **Work to ensure channel suitability.** It is important that go-to-market models reflect the needs, aspirations and expectations of the target female market. Cleanliness, safety, design and style are basic considerations. Ensure too, that everyone involved in the channel is friendly, honest, empathetic and caring.

BEWARE: THE DEVIL IS IN THE DETAIL. WOMEN ARE VERY DETAIL ORIENTED. Do not attempt to hoodwink them with headline prices that are misleading. Ensure that the offer, its terms and conditions and other relevant information is communicated fully and clearly up front. Although this is practiced by most businesses, they do it primarily as legal caveats. For women, it can convey discipline, reliability and honesty.

5 **Communicate relevantly and differently.** A business targeting women as a primary customer will have to ensure that communications are not only relevant and functional, but also evoke the emotional stimuli that matter to women.

6 **Test the market and launch a proposition to commemorate an eventful day.** A proposition targeted at women to be launched on a commemorative day like mother's day, Valentine's day, international women's day or even father's day can be a useful starting point to prove the business value of such initiatives. Women have a tendency to connect emotionally to the relevance of a day more than men. Women will appreciate this much more than men.

7 **Steps to building brand loyalty. Women are more loyal customers than men.** Once they are interested in a proposition and become a customer, they will more than likely become a repeat customer. They are also less likely to switch after a poor experience that might lead them to downgrade their net promoter score. By designing retention propositions it is possible to ensure the loyalty reward value is communicated clearly and directly to women customers. They will certainly ensure that you get the full benefits of the 'network effect' by recommending your brand and propositions to their network of family, friends and co workers. Imagine the compounded multiplier effect of this on business growth and marketing activities!

Designing and crafting propositions targeted at women

Keen observation and an understanding of the many differences between men and women are critical before attempting to craft a proposition targeted primarily at women.

Women have strong interpersonal and social networking skills

Women form deeper and longer lasting relationships with their peers, friends and work mates, and market propositions can usefully leverage this aspect:

- **Social networking tools** – Actively promote a proposition through widely available social networking tools like Facebook or Twitter. If the proposition appeals then women will actively promote, recommend and refer your brand to their network.

- **Friend-get-friend offers and discounts** – Friend-get-friend marketing and viral marketing are promotional campaigns that utilize networks of friends to distribute commercial electronic messages about a product, offer, competition or website. As women are better networkers, offers of friend-get-friend discounts and promotions will succeed better, for propositions targeted at women.

- **Special proposition offers targeted to a circle or network of women** – An offer targeted at a group of women like professionals or entrepreneurs or through a local chamber of commerce can be highly effective, as women are more active and serious networkers. So any proposition targeted to a circle of women has a high propensity for adoption by that circle.

Women have superior and keener experience of all senses

It has been scientifically observed that men's senses are relatively blunt and that women have a superior and keener experience of all their senses. This has implications when marketing to women:

- **Color vis a vis the sense of sight.** Marketers need to be especially aware of what this means in terms of color for their packaging, presentations and premises. The color cannot be too loud. It should have a soothing and softening effect.

- **Sense of hearing and listening.** Sales representatives need to speak clearly, unambiguously and honestly. Any music or the jingle for your brand or retail premises should not be too loud. Keep in mind that sound volumes that are considered normal by men are often perceived as too loud by women.

WOMEN ALSO HAVE A KEENER SENSE THAN MEN, PICKING UP SOCIAL CUES, NUANCES, INTONATION, MEANING AND INTENSITY OF CONVERSATIONS. This implies that all communications across all touch points including 'above the line' communications, collateral, websites and others need to be designed to reflect this keener sense.

Women have a strong leaning towards a nurturing and caring role

Women are by nature nurturing, caring and giving: they have an almost innate unselfish ability to nurture and give to all under their care. Marketers have a tremendous opportunity to leverage this unique trait:

- **Communications and positioning.** Marketers have an opportunity to craft their communications messages to reinforce the benefits of a proposition in a way that accentuates the caring and giving traits of women.

- **Designing the propositions.** Marketers should be extremely cautious to ensure that their proposition designs are not superfluous or falsely claimed. As caring and giving that women are, they will not hesitate to forceably reject any business that positions or attempts to promote propositions that do not deliver the desired experience intended for their loved ones!

- **Customer-facing employees.** If a business plan calls for significant marketing to women then it might be in everyone's best interest to ensure that all your employees are not only friendly, courteous and professional – but also have that X-factor pertaining to empathy, kindness and caring. It is recommended to run psychometric and psychology tests for customer-facing and front-end employees, to hand pick employees with this trait.

Women have enhanced information processing capabilities

Women have a better ability to connect, correlate, compute, relate and act on information. Women think locally and rely on details and nuances for added context. Women also have the ability to rewind relevant information over and over. This ability to decipher a wider range of information has several implications for marketing:

- **Proposition design.** Pay very special attention to the details of the product design, function and style. Ensure that no hidden costs are camouflaged within the headline price. The detail-oriented nature of women means that they will shop around and seek the best value. Ensure that the pricing of a proposition and its perceived value are well communicated so that the brand and the competitiveness of a proposition are well-understood.

- **Marketing communications.** Collateral and other product information should have an appropriate level of clarity and detail. Women will notice the nuances that matter.

- **Sales and front-office employees.** Front-line staffs need pay special attention to the fact that women have a better capability of rewinding relevant information. It is imperative that sales representatives should be consistent in what they say to their women customers and not lie through to a sale.

Women have better peripheral vision

Men have a need to track, trace and navigate the path to their goal. In other words men see in a narrow field – mild tunnel vision – with greater concentration on depth.

Women, however, take in the bigger picture – literally speaking. Not only do women have literally a wider peripheral vision but women can also store for short periods at least, more relevant and random information than men. This wider peripheral vision combined with the acute sensory awareness and overall intuitiveness makes women an interesting market to target, attract, communicate to and sell. This has several implications:

- **Retail channel location and store.** The intense peripheral vision capability of women applies to the entire external and internal surroundings of a retail store, office or location. Focus should not only be at the point of sales, but attention paid to the external and surrounding areas. Most women are busy mothers, care givers to older folks or expectant mothers. What this means is that safety, cleanliness, convenience, a play area for toddlers and immediate attention are some of the key attributes that a woman customer will appreciate more than a man.

- **Marketing communications.** The intensity of focus of the core message depends on the type of media. If it is a billboard, then it is more intense versus a print advertisement. The strong peripheral vision capabilities of women will require a design and a message that communicates the big picture of the proposition.

Women will seek out comments, opinions and suggestions of others

Men are more independent in their thoughts and actions, whilst women generally seek out and are open to suggestions, comments and opinions from others. The implications of this are far ranging:

- **Proposition design.** Propositions need be designed in ways that enable customers to give feedback, and allows the business to share customers' opinions and feedback through online, print or other media. A business is in a better position to generate real buzz and excitement around a proposition if more positive opinions and feedback are communicated back to the target market. Therefore the proposition design should facilitate the capture of this feedback so that it can be communicated back to the wider target. The tools used here are not just the obvious social media tools like Twitter or Facebook, but could include free-call 800 numbers where customers can call in, as well as micro-sites specifically created and targeted for the launch of a single proposition.

- **Marketing communications.** Use of 'real world' testimonials would certainly be effective when targeted at women. This has the compounded effect of creating and communicating a personalized message for potential women customers.

All this advice should be relevant and applicable when marketing to any target. The point being made here is to highlight the differences between men and women and its relevance to the marketing and design of propositions targeted to women.

AMERICAN AUTHOR CAMILLE PAGLIA once said, "Women are in league with each other, a secret conspiracy of hearts and pheromones". Woe betide any marketer who fails to understand the consequence of this.

NOTES

SECTION

4

KEY CONSIDERATIONS FOR MANAGING AND OPERATING YOUR BUSINESS

THE UNCERTAINTY THAT
REMAINS AFTER THE BEST
POSSIBLE ANALYSIS HAS
BEEN UNDERTAKEN, IS WHAT
MCKINSEY CALLS RESIDUAL
UNCERTAINTY.

A SIMPLE FRAMEWORK
FOR LESS COMPLEX BUSINESS
DECISION-MAKING

Understanding McKinsey's 'residual uncertainty' theory and applying it in real life

Business owners, investors and managers can be faced with a multitude of options and choices and many of us will have made major or minor decisions at some point in our business or personal life that we have regretted later.

Be it an investment choice, a major purchase, a hiring choice, a major price cut, a key strategic investment or other daily business or personal decisions or strategies, we will all from time to time wish that we have the gift and wisdom of foresight.

In the US it's referred to as 20/20 hindsight. The notion is that by looking back to the past (hindsight), we can see what and how something went wrong – and hopefully learn from that experience and understand how to tackle the situation better next time. In the same way that perfect vision is 20/20, with 20/20 hindsight we are able to see perfectly what should have been done to produce the best outcome.

So how does this help us deal with uncertainty in the business world?

Most business schools teach some level of managerial decision-making, as well as how to use the various tools and frameworks that aid in decision making. On a personal level, any discussion of strategy or uncertainties always brings to mind an excellent *McKinsey Quarterly* article of a decade or so ago that dealt with different levels and types of uncertainty. This article had a profound influence on the way I look at uncertainty in my personal or professional life.

In essence, the article stated that most strategically relevant information falls into one of two categories of structured and residual factors.

- Often it is possible to identify clear trends like demographics and macro economic data. Further, with the right level of due diligence and analysis, most remaining unknown factors could be determined through **structured analysis.** These include the likes of technology risks, market risks, financial risks and other risks like supply and demand-side factors such as competitor responses, customer adoption rates including potential elasticity to price reduction, and financing coverage capability from cash flows generated.

- The uncertainty that remains after the best possible analysis has been undertaken, is what McKinsey calls **residual uncertainty**. Examples of this include the outcome of a legal suit, outcomes of regulatory changes, or the performance attributes of a nascent technology that has not been fully deployed or adopted, or one that is still under development. These residual uncertainties can be classified into four levels.

BY LIMITING THEIR STRATEGIC ANALYSIS TO LEVEL 1 UNCERTAINTY, telecommunications managers are therefore in danger of drawing the wrong conclusions.

1. **Level I uncertainty – Easy choices** In level 1 uncertainty the possible outcome is known, so no multi-scenario analysis is required. But we must be sure that decision-making required on a residual uncertainty is really a level one uncertainty. In the telecommunications industry for instance, most business decisions or strategies are facing uncertainties beyond level 1 simply because of the fast pace of change in that sector.

2. Level 2 uncertainty – Multiple choices and alternative outcomes In level 2 uncertainty, we can expect one of a few discrete scenarios. In essence it accepts that any analysis cannot predict absolute outcomes, and requires us to assign probabilities of alternative outcomes based on the best information, tools and knowledge available.

A classic level 2 situation is currently playing out in several telecom sectors as operators decide on how best to invest in the upgrades from 2G to full 3G and then onto 4G. In this scenario telecom players are being forced to make the high stake multi-billion investments, even when the previous generation technologies have not generated the desired returns. The value of this type of investments is partly dependent on their market competitors' investment strategies, which cannot yet be observed or predicted.

If the first mover invests in a higher performance technology, others in the market will be forced to invest to minimize their opportunity costs or face a high probability of customer churn and rapid per unit revenue degradation.
The possible outcomes and moves of the competitor are discrete and clear – Will they invest, yes or no, and if yes, when? The best strategy depends on which one does, and when it happens.

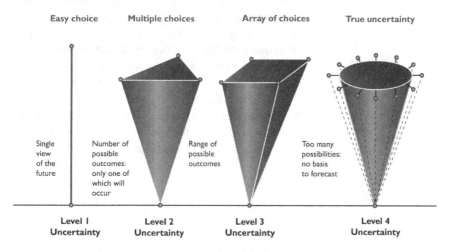

Figure 21: A framework to better understand the different levels of uncertainty.

3. **Level three – Array of choices** In level 3, there are a range of possible outcomes that can be identified, with very few variables. A good example of a level 3 uncertainty is when a telecom operator in a small market has to make a choice as to, if and when to align with Mobile Virtual Network Operators (MVNOs are companies that provide mobile phone services but do not have their own spectrum and usually do not have their own network infrastructure). The significant factors that determine this sort of strategy have multiple levels of uncertainty – ranging from the decision to align with an MVNO or not to, to the level of pricing, the cannibalization of revenue and customer issues, whether to limit the sales to a niche segment or to the broader market. Additional considerations could include the level of costs and customer control to be transferred to the MVNO. It will require a detailed, structured and multi-scenario analysis to address this, and it will often be a complex and arduous task to predict the outcome of this type of uncertainty.

Any scenario development should facilitate easy decision making. Therefore, it is recommended that the number of scenarios be limited, should not overlap and each have unique implications.

4. **Level 4 – True uncertainty** A level 4 uncertainty is truly ambiguous. It is hard to predict the outcomes. Level 4 uncertainties are rare in most industries, but do exist in fast-moving sectors like media, ICT and the telecommunications industry where the emergence of the multiple VoIP players like Skype or Rebtel and other digital media companies like Google and Facebook are proving hugely disruptive. No amount of analysis could have actually predicted in 2002 or 2003, the outcome of how and when they will wreck the telecom player's voice business (the real gravy for the telecoms industry and the killer app of all time). Today, the outcomes seem a little too obvious. Yes, hindsight is indeed 20/20.

DEVELOPING A SET OF SCENARIOS should at the least enable managers to assess the wisdom of their existing or planned status quo strategies.

Level 4 uncertainty in practise

Take a company like Vodafone. Its Western European revenues are declining. It has invested billions in 3G and next generation networks and acquired many developing market telecom players to offset the anticipated decline in revenue from its developed markets portfolio. The cash flow growths in these newly acquired companies are coming under heavy pressure due to the significant price reductions as the operators try to boost market adoption. Additionally, all the players in the telecommunications value chain are forcing them to expend or reinvest their free cash flow.

The processor core and network vendors are upgrading their network equipment. Further, all it takes is an "irrational" player in any of their markets to force them to prematurely invest billions in the network.

The advent of new smart phones like the iPhone are forcing them to subsidize the handsets and the network just to retain their existing base. The MVNOs are forcing them to drop prices just to stay competitive. Multiple content players are forcing them to rethink and invest heavily in their networks and data strategy. The new media players like Skype and Google are forcing them to reduce their voice prices. The regulators are pressurizing them to reduce prices on their high-margin roaming propositions. Informed individual customers and enterprises are demanding the best deal and the lowest prices. On top of all these factors, imagine the range of new organizational capabilities required to transform the company into a nimble new age media player.

- **How does the company justify the growth assumptions** that have been baked into its enterprise valuation?
- **How and where does it shape,** adapt or reserve the right to play?
- **What are the portfolio of strategies,** initiatives, actions, big bet moves, options and no regret plays that Vodafone should be embarking on?

Vodafone's management and shareholders are surely facing a level 4 uncertainty.

Shape or be shaped!

Addressing level 4 uncertainties requires a player to shape or be shaped, be prepared to adapt or reserve the right to play. The choice of strategies to address level 4 uncertainties are dependent on the extent of competitive leverage, the risk averseness of the management and its financial strength, and a multitude of other factors like investor appetite, organizational capability, innovation orientation and so on. Assigning informed and reasonable probabilities will help us develop investment and pricing plans and product portfolio rebalancing strategies, that are phased to ensure that they don't end up being the proverbial 'dumb pipe'.

Don't let your foresight be blind!

The range of the levels of uncertainty can stretch from a broad spectrum of one of two possible outcomes to a wholly unknown and ambiguous set of variables.

Knowing the levels of uncertainty, and being able to think purposefully and in a structured way through the multiple scenarios and probabilities and the strategies to address these uncertainties, is an essential skill for any manager.

Understanding and addressing the levels of uncertainty is the only way to avoid Monday morning quarter backing... The methods described here can be applied to both your professional and personal life... Hindsight is 20/20. Don't let your foresight be blind!

NOTES

DONE WELL, ICT DEPLOYMENT SHOULD ENABLE A BUSINESS TO LOWER ITS COSTS AND IMPROVE BUSINESS PROCESS AS WELL AS PEOPLE EFFICIENCY AND EFFECTIVENESS.

ICT INVESTMENT FOR BUSINESS VALUE CREATION

Managing ICT solutions carefully and top tips for choosing the right partners

All businesses from time to time will be pressed for cash flow, and there are market mechanisms now in place in many regions that could help ensure that business capital expenditure investments in ICT are funded by the providers of the ICT services rather than the business user. Included in these are:

- Managed ICT solutions that are delivered as an on-line service.
- On-demand or utility computing which is billed as a variable monthly expense.
- Out-tasking of must-have ICT functions that are non-core or commodity procedures like IT support, anti-virus and anti-spam information security assurance, or service desk call center operations.

These are all means through which businesses can avoid capital expenditure and move ICT towards an operating expense model that runs in parallel with the demands of the business and has reduced impact on cash flow because capital expenditure is avoided. For all the right reasons, they are set to be as popular with businesses as office block rental schemes or car lease programs have become.

ICT Cost Analysis

In-house	vs	Outsourcing

In-house	Outsourcing
• On-payroll labor costs over two or three shifts	• 24 x 7 coverage
	• Cash-flow benefits
• Hardware depreciation	• Capex avoidance
• Software licenses	• Access to latest software versions with automatic upgrades
• Facilities costs	• Service cost transparency/visibility
• Hire/retain expenses	• Lower Total Cost of Ownership (TCO)
• Payroll / HR administration	
• Lost opportunity costs	• Service Level Assurance (SLA) geared to minimize business downtime
• Training costs	• Regulatory assurances
• Cost of compliance with regulatory obligations	• Services continually enhanced to meet regulatory mandates

Figure 22: A clear and careful ICT Cost Analysis will help SME owners identify areas for resource deployment.

The ICT awareness and needs of businesses are diverse and disparate, and many smaller businesses in particular can feel that any investment in ICT is costly and does not generate the requisite returns. This is certainly not true. Done well, ICT deployment should enable a business to lower its costs, improve business process and people efficiency and effectiveness, and in many cases can actually help generate more revenue. In fact, ICT investments are a paramount requirement to increased productivity – and bearing in mind that a 10% increase in productivity can sometimes determine whether a business remains competitive and sustainable, the successful and economic deployment of ICT must be deemed critical to business success.

This can be a problem for the smaller business, which lacks the ICT expertise necessary to undertake major deployments and ICT-led projects without resorting to costly consulting and external support. So it is imperative that SMBs select an ICT partner that is reliable, knowledgeable and offers the best value for money.

A-B-C of selecting an ICT partner

Every business seeks superior value for money, and in the context of ICT services this means pricing predictability and an operating transparency of the supplier that promises value, convenience and ease of use. There are three simple A-B-C steps to follow that will help in the selection of an ICT provider, and which help ensure the correct level of focus on value, predictability of use and convenience.

Accessibility and convenience

Is the ICT supplier able to provide a complete solution, and pull together everything that is needed for the deployment or project? Can they provide a one-stop shop, rather than the business having to separately source additional systems or equipment from other providers?

Business model

Does the commercial framework of the provider offer a means of shifting away from Capex investment towards the Opex operating cost model, which helps balance outgoings in line with the actual usage of the ICT systems being deployed? Is the pricing transparent and predictable?

Complexity

Does the provider take away from the business or reduce some of the complexity of deployment or use of ICT? Does it do away with the need of having internal resources managing and maintaining it, so that every employee is focused on running the business supported by the best ICT tools and services?

I **Value for money** Working capital management is critical for all businesses but for SMBs an optimal working capital management could make the difference between survival or closure of the business. Therefore, as part of the proposition for ICT value for money, any offer should require minimal capital outlay requirements. Instead, the offer should minimize the call on capital expenditure (Capex) and shift the cost of ICT ownership towards an operational expenditure (Opex) model, with minimal financing costs. Cash is king and these schemes are by far the best option.

2 Predictability of use Few SMBs have the necessary resources or internal know-how to handle a LAN installation, or carry our network management or database administration tasks, or manage security or storage requirements, which are among the many other critical IT functions and elements that large businesses take for granted. The opportunity costs of hiring a specialist with the requisite IT skills are high. When selecting a provider, it is critical they are able to offer their services on a pay-as-you-use model albeit on a per employee basis, per seat, per month, per port basis, or any other per unit basis.

3 Convenience The wide and complex array of solutions, systems and sub systems mean that most businesses without the prerequisite know-how and skills are not only confused but easily overwhelmed by the multitude of choices and proposals being offered to them. Crucially, a supplier's proposition should be a one-stop economical solution. This is not to say that we should accept an ICT provider offering a one-size-fits-all proposition. Today there is a broad set of established and emerging players in many regions that are offering niche and differentiated propositions, solutions and services tailored to suit the special needs of the smaller business.

WHEN SELECTING CALLING PLANS from providers, it's worth checking they do not mix peak, off peak and different country rates. For most SMBs, any day and any time is peak for business.

BUSINESS MOBILITY

Research indicates the SMB segment requires value-driven, simple to understand and predictable mobile offers that meet varied calling pattern needs, and a certain level of user sophistication. Key requirements have been driven by a need for competitive international calling rates, special calling rates within the business, international roaming benefits and a choice of smart phones with a low Capex commercial model.

BUSINESS FIXED VOICE SERVICES

SMBs need a reliable and cost-effective fixed-line service that meets their immediate and growth requirements. Key requirements include significant savings on international and national calls. Look for a voice service provider that enables customers direct access to your employees, and offers a variety of calling features like call forwarding and three-way calling. Look for usage offers, where the more you use, the more you save.

BUSINESS BROADBAND SERVICES

Volume-based usage billing is slowly ebbing away globally, giving way to unlimited usage packages. Unlimited usage comes with predictable costs which can be built into a SMB's Opex budget. Key requirements include bundled benefits that offer significant savings on the overall telecommunication spend.

MANAGED SERVICES

Doing more with less remains the perennial challenge for organizations of any size. That challenge has special significance for IT departments, as the race to keep up with advancing technology gets more complex and critical every day. Businesses need to focus on their core strength and there is a growing trend globally as well as in the UAE to outsource non-core business functions, including ICT. Research indicates that more than 40% of business customers look upon their telecommunications provider as an experienced and reliable partner to handle end-to-end ICT needs, which includes core telecom services as well as non-core telecom services such as IT security, network management, hosting services, storage, back-up and software applications.

BUSINESS CONTINUITY SERVICES

Business continuity requirements and cost controls typically drive the decision to use managed services, and businesses are increasingly moving towards managed and hosted models. Most SMEs never really know nor understand the impact which data loss can have on their business. Viruses, theft, hard drive crashes, and accidental file deletion can happen at any time and put any businesses future in danger. There are solutions that ICT providers have which will safeguard files and drives, and whether it is automatic storage, backup or virus-prevention there is a large suite of cost-effective solutions to defend against cyber damage. A preferred provider has to understand a customer's security needs, and should have partnered with leading security brands to provide products specially developed with SMBs in mind. Scalable products are available, which provide businesses with a capability to add as much storage and units as are needed at any time, changes can be made whenever they need be, multi-user environments managed, automatic backups scheduled, and the health of the backups and computers monitored from the convenience of a web-based console.

WITH THE IMPENDING OPENING UP OF MANY MARKETS FOR TELECOM OPERATORS SOON, business customers can look forward to great offers and packages in the fixed broadband arena as it is now in the business mobility arena.

Getting more business bang for the ICT buck

The imperative with business ICT is to make a smart choice of provider, one that is able to supply a complete package which has been designed with the unique needs of the business in mind.

Look for a partner that has a reputable brand, is considered innovative, dynamic and flexible, and one with the financial muscle to survive and prosper by serving you better over the long term.

Start with the A-B-C: Is the proposition convenient and delivered as a complete solution? Is the commercial model correct? Does it remove complexity? If the answer is yes to all three, expect a bigger bang from the ICT buck.

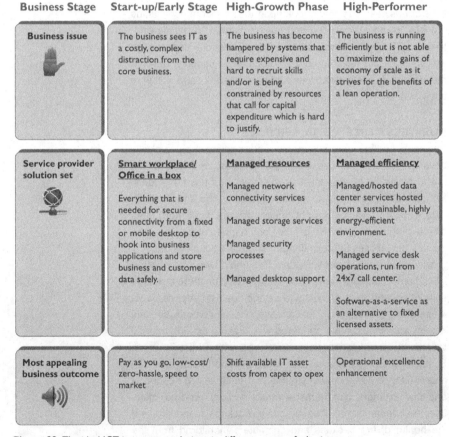

Business Stage	Start-up/Early Stage	High-Growth Phase	High-Performer
Business issue	The business sees IT as a costly, complex distraction from the core business.	The business has become hampered by systems that require expensive and hard to recruit skills and/or is being constrained by resources that call for capital expenditure which is hard to justify.	The business is running efficiently but is not able to maximize the gains of economy of scale as it strives for the benefits of a lean operation.
Service provider solution set	**Smart workplace/ Office in a box** Everything that is needed for secure connectivity from a fixed or mobile desktop to hook into business applications and store business and customer data safely.	**Managed resources** Managed network connectivity services Managed storage services Managed security processes Managed desktop support	**Managed efficiency** Managed/hosted data center services hosted from a sustainable, highly energy-efficient environment. Managed service desk operations, run from 24x7 call center. Software-as-a-service as an alternative to fixed licensed assets.
Most appealing business outcome	Pay as you go, low-cost/ zero-hassle, speed to market	Shift available IT asset costs from capex to opex	Operational excellence enhancement

Figure 23: The ideal ICT investment solutions in different stages of a business.

How to identify your perfect ICT partner

Accessibility and convenience	Is the ICT supplier able to provide a complete solution, and pull together everything that is needed for the deployment or project? Can they provide a one-stop shop, rather than the business having to separately source additional systems or equipment from other providers?
Business model	Does the commercial framework of the provider offer a means of shifting away from Capex investment towards the Opex operating cost model, which helps balance outgoings in line with the actual usage of the ICT systems being deployed? Is the pricing transparent and predictable?
Complexity	Does the provider take away from the business or reduce some of the complexity of deployment or use of ICT? Does it do away with the need of having internal resources managing and maintaining it, so that every employee is focused on running the business supported by the best ICT tools and services?

Figure 24: Make sure you tick all these boxes and get more business bang for the ICT buck.

NOTES

PLEASE ENSURE THAT YOUR ENTIRE CRITICAL CUSTOMER, SUPPLIER, EMPLOYEE AND OTHER INFORMATION ARE REGULARLY BACKED UP.

MANAGING YOUR BUSINESS OPERATIONS

Step-by-step guide to good operations management that will allow your business to flourish

Every business has an operational aspect to it. Whether you are running and managing a restaurant or a retail business, the manner in which you run your operations can determine whether your business is profitable and sustainable.

Most SME owners and investors do not pay any attention to this critical aspect of their business.

Definition of operations management

My definition of operations management is that it includes the formulation, design, planning, process mapping, execution and the control of operations to convert all your resources into products, services and/or goods. In other words, the operations management is how you execute on your intended business strategy. The resources could range from your human, financial, inventory, capacity and or any resources deployed to create incremental value.

THE LIST OF OPERATIONAL ISSUES that I will discuss in this chapter is by no means mutually exclusive nor are they completely exhaustive.

Most operational management issues discussed here would seem very obvious to you. However, you will be surprised to note how few small businesses really pay heed to these obvious management issues. Otherwise, we would not often hear of theft, vandalism, lack of inventory or stock and poor after sales and/or customer service in many SMEs.

A note on policy, procedure and process and system

Having a policy, procedures and processes will significantly help a small business to combine a documented system under which the small business will operate.

Policy – A policy can either be written or be a verbal statement of a small business' stance on an issues or topic. It helps the SME owner to define how things are done in his or her business and what rules apply to the respective stakeholders. Policies can include such things as annual leave, payment to suppliers, overtime, dress code, internet usage and others in the workplace.

Procedure – A procedure is a step-by-step instruction to achieve a certain outcome of the business. Some procedures are general whilst others must be detailed. A manufacturing process or the handling of work place injuries or the operation of the factory machinery or heavy equipment must be detailed and written by an expert.

Process and system – A process is a method or system for achieving a certain outcome for your small business. The process should be repeatable and structured. In other words, you cannot have different processes and ways every other day. The process should ensure that nepotism (in hiring), fraud, theft, verification and checks and controls are in place so that no one or two persons can jeopardize your business. However, checks and controls should not create unnecessary layers of bureaucracy that will affect your service to your customers. It is important for small business owners that company policies, procedures and processes are properly documented and can easily be understood and made available to all relevant employees. An important note on employment contracts – When policies, procedures or processes form part of your small business employee's terms and conditions of employment, they must be attached or linked to the employment contract.

Six key benefits of a documented system

- Consistency in the delivery of customer experience across all touch points
- Smooth operations of the small business
- Lack of dependency on the owner for the running of the business
- Faster and easier exit for the owner
- Reduction of overall risk to the small business
- Enables training of employees

Process mapping

It is important that you, as a small business owner or manager, have a defined process (not necessarily documented in a binder that no one reads) that your employees and you can follow for critical processes like:

- Hiring
- Ordering and receiving inventory
- Supplier payment
- Inventory management

- Production or service methods
- Sales and marketing
- Cash handling
- Salary payments

Key operational management issues to which a small business should pay special attention

WORKPLACE SECURITY

It is imperative that you should first and foremost address the safety and security of your business, your employees and customers. You should put preventive measures to mitigate risks of fraud, theft and vandalism so as to ensure that your small business' assets, inventory and machinery, and other critical assets vital to the running of your business, are not jeopardized.

You should conduct a thorough assessment and contingency plan to help minimize losses due to:

- Fire
- Burglary
- Fraud
- Injury to your employees

DATA STORAGE AND BACK UP

Please ensure that your entire critical customer, supplier, employee and other information are regularly backed up. I have personally seen many small businesses incur significant losses by not paying attention to this one issue.

INTERNET FRAUD

As our digital lives are a matter of fact, please pay special attention to Internet fraud or online fraud schemes that use email, websites, chat rooms or message boards to represent your company or you for fraudulent solicitations and/or transactions. Pay special attention to your online cash transfer process and verification.

Watch out for disgruntled employees or others installing spyware into your computer systems to takes things from you without you even knowing about it.

If you have personal customer information stored in your computer systems, watch out phishing from within or outside your company.

PHISHING is a technique used to gain personal information for the purpose of identity theft.

ADMINISTRATION MANAGEMENT

Small business owners often do not pay any attention to the administration and management of their business. As a small business owner, you should be acutely aware and comply with reporting and record-keeping obligations that you might have.

As a small business owner, you will have to pay special attention to the process mapping and administration management of a few critical areas:

- **Financial management** – Ensure that your small business accounts payable and receivable management, the preparation of financial statements, budget planning and reporting processes are structured and well understood by your employees.

- **Business compliance requirements** – Ensure that all regulatory and governmental compliance requirements are met. These could range from ensuring that there is adequate insurance, tax withholding, payment of social security tax, transportation records and employee visas and details. If for some unfortunate reason your firm is audited by any governmental or regulatory authorities, you will be mired in countless hours trying to prove that you are in full compliance. Remember that the onus is almost always on you! Therefore, pay special attention to record keeping, which includes, but is not limited to, filing, collecting information on business issues and maintaining statutory documentation.

- **Database management systems and process** – Ensure that you have abundant and reliable database management systems and processes to accurately track your customers, suppliers and competitors.

- **Human resources and people issues** – Ensure that the administration of supervising your employees and maintaining records of their payroll and sick days and vacations are proper and correct.

- **Office equipment and supplies' purchases and maintenance** – Ensure that processes are in place to maximize the productivity of your employees. I have seen many businesses not having adequate supplies and wherein employees often end up wasting time until supplies or equipment are replenished or replaced.

- **Supplier management and contracting** – Most small businesses ignore supplier management and legal contract issues to their own detriment. Pay special attention to mitigate fraud and overcharging and/or potential legal suits down the road.

- **Outsourcing** – Small businesses should consider outsourcing as a viable option if too much time is spent on administration of a specific process or task. Administration issues often distract a SME owner or manager and take up invaluable time that should be spent on running the core operations of the business. It is therefore imperative to create systems, methods, processes and procedures to increase productivity of your employees and cut unnecessary repetition and wasting of valuable time and resources.

MOST SMALL BUSINESSES FACE CRITICAL SUPPLY CHAIN MANAGEMENT ISSUES when the business is growing. These challenges and issues often lead to a decrease in productivity, increased costs and lower customer satisfaction.

SUPPLY CHAIN & LOGISTICS MANAGEMENT

Every small business, irrespective of the industry, has a supply chain. Supply chain management includes the management of all tasks and activities to transform the raw materials, service or products into a customer value proposition and includes ensuring that these services and products are delivered to the customer. It also includes the management of processes and system for assembling, storing and disposing of waste materials for your finished customer value proposition.

Many small businesses pay little or no attention to end-to-end performance reporting for their business. Remember always that what you cannot measure, you cannot report; and what you cannot report, you cannot manage. If you cannot manage something, you definitely don't have the chance to improve performance.

The critical elements of a supply chain management system

- Selecting suppliers – single and multiple
- Procurement
- Managing lead times for inventory
- Managing supplier relationships
- Production or service planning
- Inventory management
- Procurement and purchasing
- Customer service management
- Inventory and distribution management of returned or faulty goods

Inventory management

Excessive inventories lead to additional costs or wastage that your small business cannot afford. Lack of inventories could mean order cancellations and customer dissatisfaction. Budget furcating and planning are critical to ensure that your small business has the optimal inventory at all times.

Performance reporting

Your operations management should have process and systems that accurately report the performance of your business. This includes:

- Employee performance and other employee issues such as sick leave, vacation and others
- Customer activity
- Sales performance
- Product performance
- Performance of your factory or major assets
- Stock and Inventory
- Financial performance
- Customer service performance
- Cash flow and float
- Supplier performance
- Computer and telecommunications systems

Summary

Operations management is an important aspect of your business. It is often mundane and basic common sense. Many small business owners pay scant attention to this critical aspect of their business. Your failure to pay special attention to this important aspect of your business could mean lost customers and profits. In simple words, what this means is that the prudent management, or the lack thereof, of the operations of your small business could determine whether your business flourishes or perishes.

I want to leave you with a final thought on operations management. In the end, all business operations could be summarized into 3 areas: people, propositions and profits. Unless you have a grip on the operations of your small business, all three areas of your business will be impacted.

On that note, here is a quote from Scott Allen "a project is complete when it starts working for you, rather than you working for it".

NOTES

SECTION

MANAGEMENT STRATEGIES TO GROW YOUR BUSINESS

TRYING TO SOLVE ALL MAJOR ISSUES AT ONE TIME WITHOUT FOCUSING ON A FEW CRITICAL ONES IS OFTEN COSTLY AND NON-ATTAINABLE AND ALMOST ALWAYS FUTILE AND LEADS TO FAILURE.

THE ART OF FOCUS: FUNDAMENTAL MATH FOR BUSINESS

How to apply the Pareto Principle in business and help it grow to its full potential

Focusing on the details of the business is vitally important, but it is wise also to focus on the details that matter and to try understand the power of the Pareto principle.

Sometimes referred to as the Pareto efficiency, the 80-20 rule, the law of the vital few or the principle of factor sparsity, Pareto states that for many events, roughly 80% of the effects come from 20% of the causes. Business management thinker Joseph M. Juran proposed the principle, naming it after Italian economist Vilfredo Pareto, who observed in 1906 that 80% of the land in Italy was owned by 20% of the population. (He developed the principle by observing that 20% of the pea pods in his garden contained 80% of the peas.) Day in and day out, business people barely give it a thought, overlook its significance and only rarely apply this 'universal' cardinal to improve their business efficiency, productivity and profitability.

Actual Sales Performance

Figure 25: An 'average' means nothing and is totally misleading, as this illustration proves.

The fallacy of averages

Every day in business the talk is of the average sales per day being so much, or the average revenue per customer being that. Others often talk about the average returns of the stock market, or the average number of days in a delivery cycle. But averages mean nothing. Imagine a plane flying from a to b and the average terrain is 3000 feet, calculated from a low of 0 feet above sea level and a mountain peak of 6000 feet. You can just imagine if the pilot decides to plot his flight plan based on an average of 3000 feet. Or, imagine a person with no swimming skills trying to cross a lake just because some one said that the average depth is 3 feet. Averages are fallacies in real life, and also in business.

A focus on the fallacy of 'average sales' can mask poor performance and star achievers

Trying to understand the business by discussing averages will provide little insight if the average revenue derived from a few customers is exponentially bigger than the rest. In the telecommunications industry, we focus long and hard on the average revenue per customer, the average minutes of use, the average orders per channel, or the average customer care service levels. These averages are useless and baseless. They reveal nothing about the business because the average revenue might be inflated as a result of having a few large customers, versus the rest of the base. Imagine building capacity for a mobile phone network, factory, hotel, or a restaurant based on averages. A restaurant that has excellent food falls down if service is very poor during peak times. In most companies, 80% of the incremental sales (new sales) are generated through about 20% of the sales folks. Still most training investments are spread across the entire sales force. Just imagine the returns if a company could hone that to the next 5th or 10th percentile; imagine the tremendous results that could be achieved, and the savings to be made when we focus on the details that matter. Try saying to an employee that the average bonus payout is $X, when he or she probably received one fifth of that $X. The average is as close to the bottom, as it is to the top.

AS THE FAMOUS US STAND-UP COMEDIAN GEORGE CARLIN ONCE SAID, "Just think of how stupid the average person is, and then realise half of them are even stupider!" Focusing on the averages really mean nothing.

Pareto, laser focus and the '64-4' law

If a result, problem, outcome or anything has 80% of effects coming from 20% of causes, it follows that the 80% of that top 80% of effects come from 20% of that top 20% of causes, and so on (80% of 80% is 64%; 20% of 20% is 4% – so there is a '64/4' law to explore here). Often, just by knowing that 4% of customers, revenues, problems or issues could be much more worth your attention than all the others put together, is good enough to make a difference to business. It does not always have to add up to 100 (80/20), it could be 70/40 in that 70% of a company's revenue comes from 40% of its customers. The key is to focus on what matters. Trying to solve all major issues at one time without focusing on a few critical ones is often costly and non-attainable and almost always futile and leads to failure.

The application of the Pareto principles doesn't have to be restricted to business, but rather can be applied to everyday living. Imagine if you are trying to save money or if something or some one annoys you, or that you feel 'good' only on certain occasions. Just focusing on the few issues or attributes or behaviors that matter can help address, alleviate or enhance the experience or relationship, or whatever it is that you are trying to do. The Pareto Principle is a 'power law' relationship, a special kind of mathematical relationship between two quantities. When the frequency of an event varies as a power of some attribute of that event (eg its size), the frequency is said to follow a power law. The distribution of a wide variety of natural and man-made phenomena follow a power law, including frequencies of words in most languages, frequencies of family names, sizes of craters on the moon and of solar flares, the sizes of power outages, earthquakes, and wars, the popularity of books and music, and many other quantities.

Stay focused: Life is too short

We need to thank Mr Pareto for a universal principle that can be applied in our everyday life. It might seem too obvious or easy, but most folks ignore this principle day in and day out. Just observe this at work where people in Finance, Sales, HR, Technology, Operations and Marketing will all be preaching about the average of this and that. Take note and decide if it makes sense. Force the discussions around the stuff that really matters.

NOTES

I SET MYSELF UP AS A COACH AND FACILITATOR, RATHER THAN A MANAGER, FOR MY TEAM. I SEE IT AS MY RESPONSIBILITY TO ENABLE MY TEAM'S SUCCESS.

23

THE MAKING OF A GOOD MANAGER

Ancient and modern definitions of a manager – and how you can become a great one

People are by far and away the single biggest asset of any business, and every business owner/manager will want to take their responsibility as a 'manager of people' very seriously indeed. Management style is an evolutionary and transformational process, and there are lessons that can be learned that will help ensure you always get the very best from your team. (Personally, there were some early periods in my career where when only results mattered and that the 'means justified the end'. There were also times where the full frailties of humankind were depicted to the teams that I managed. Anger, impatience, suspicion, insecurity, threats and other mortal sins were among some of the characteristics displayed. I still get angry and impatient, though much less frequently!)

Formally, 'management' (from Old French ménagement 'the art of conducting, directing', from Latin manuagere' to lead by the hand') characterises the process of leading and directing all or any part of an organization, often a business, through the deployment and manipulation of human, financial, material, intellectual or intangible resources. This definition was definitely written a very long time ago. In this fast moving world of ours, even a hint of trying to 'lead someone by the hand' especially a bright, educated and intelligent graduate will not get you any where fast. It fact, this notion of leading by hand could actually be counterproductive to attaining the desired goals and results. Indeed, one assumption I now make, is that everyone in the team is smarter than me! That said, another assumption is that as a manager I must have the requisite knowledge and experience until proven otherwise. So I set myself up as a coach and facilitator, rather than a manager, for my team. I see it as my responsibility to enable my team's success. So what is a good approach to management?

HONESTY NEEDS TO BE PRACTICED EVERY DAY. Flattery and false praises will be seen through by smart people.

Honesty – We have to be honest with our teams. We should openly praise and recognize the team or individuals for their achievements. A manager should openly credit his or her team for recognition of any success that the team has achieved. A manager should never take credit for the work done by their team, but should give full praise and credit to the team. (Of course the manager will have to take the blame when things go wrong – that's the irony of management!). At the same time, a good coach and facilitator should be honest even when things are not going well or when improvement is required of someone. They should provide open and frank feedback, guidance and mentoring. They should also be ready to raise the stakes to the extent of openly chiding the employee, so as to send a message to everyone that a certain behavior is and will not be tolerated

Understanding and respecting different points of reference – All men and women are equal, but we are not created equal. In any international team, it is obvious that we all come from very different cultural, religious and social backgrounds, with different beliefs and values. Recognizing that in a team there might be different functional specialties, different education, interests and backgrounds, is crucial to success as a manager. Trying to understand and respect the unique characteristics of each team member is important, if the different perspectives they bring is to be fully appreciated and valued.

Empathy – Before we are employees or managers or workers, we are first and foremost human beings. Therefore it is important to connect with people on a personal basis. Showing genuine interest and concern in team members' family, education, hobbies and other personal interests will be appreciated by every one. Showing understanding and genuine concern when something is personally affecting an employee will never be forgotten by them.

Results do matter – We are all employees in a for-profit corporation to generate results that will generate profits. We have an obligation to the company and its shareholders to deliver results. As a manager you will be judged on your results. It is your team's efforts that generate the results that you are measured and paid against. An acute awareness of this helps, and any lack of understanding of this critical element will be fatal to your career!

SHARE THE JOYS AND MISERIES of everyday living with your team. You will be appreciated for it.

The test of goodness, truthfulness and usefulness

So do you pass the test of goodness, truthfulness and usefulness? (This is a quote borrowed from a CEO that I admire a lot, and said in a different context in a recent meeting). To be a good manager, you will have to pass all the three elements of this test.

1 **Goodness** – Do you have empathy for your team? Do you connect to people? In other words, are you human? Do you appreciate and recognize the different points of reference that each of us has?

2 **Truthfulness** – Are you truthful to your team? Are you honest to yourself?

3 **Usefulness** – We are all corporate warriors for a purpose – to be useful and deliver results.

So are you truly useful? Pass all three tests and you can consider yourself to be a good coach and facilitator; you cannot add value for your shareholders without adding value to your employees first

NOTES

A DISCIPLINED AND DELIBERATE APPLICATION OF THE LINCOLN 6PS IS POWERFULLY COHESIVE, BY MAKING EVERYONE INVOLVED FEEL LIKE PEAS IN A POD!

A SIMPLE FRAMEWORK FOR A SMARTER EVERYDAY BUSINESS MANAGEMENT

Adopt the easy-to-follow Lincoln 6Ps and take your business to the next level

Most of us will have heard about the 4Ps of marketing (Product, Price, Promotion and Place), or the McKinsey 7-S value-based management framework for organizational effectiveness (Structure, Strategy, Systems, Skills, Style, Staff and Shared values). The good folks in brand and communications have the 7Ps of branding (Profit, Persistence, Planning, Performance, Positioning, People and Principles), and there are no doubt numerous others that offer guidance to other parts of the business.

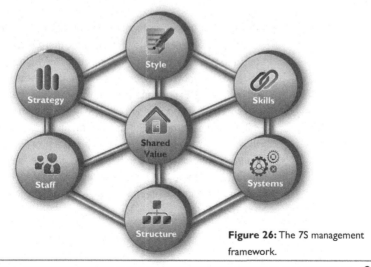

Figure 26: The 7S management framework.

Figure 27: Other examples of workable marketing frameworks.

Whilst all of these are highly relevant and reliable frameworks developed by real experts in their fields, there is a much simpler and easy to remember framework that will help us get to the very heart of how every business manager needs to do the 'art of business.' Experience has shown that this framework can be successfully applied in almost every situation, campaign or initiative. The 'Lincoln Ps' are not mutually exclusive, nor are they completely exhaustive. They are a set of Ps from various sources made relevant, ordered and framed as an easy to remember framework that will address most management issues, ranging from day-to-day activities to implementing large-scale projects.

THE LINCOLN PS – PURPOSE

What is the objective or purpose of a certain initiative, campaign or tactic? There has to be a central issue or objective that can be planned for, communicated, executed on and expected as an outcome. There may be multiple other significant factors that should or might be considered, however, there can only be one single central issue.

PROFIT

Is there a profit to be made? Do the profits meet the required hurdle rates? Is it feasible? If some thing supposedly generates a high value, but its feasibility or probability of execution is low, then it is not profitable. Are short-term profits, cash flow or positioning-for-growth important? If these questions can be answered honestly, we can determine if the initiative will be profitable or not.

Figure 28: The *Lincoln 6Ps* in the pod: easy and effective.

PLAN

Planning! Planning! Planning! The success of any initiative, campaign or tactic is buried in the detail: do we have a feasible plan to implement our initiative? Have we taken contingencies into account for the campaign? Does our tactic require multi-scenario planning and, if so, do we have one in place?

PROCESS

How are we going to get our plan implemented? Is there a set of systems and processes that we can rely on to deliver or implement the plan? Are the existing governance processes adequate to get resources, and manage, track and report progress of the implementation?

CONVERSELY, it is easy for ideas to lose momentum if they are under-communicated, and which means there is very little buy-in in place.

PACE

How are we going to communicate the details and progress of our initiative? Who are we going to communicate to? What level of details will we communicate? Do we have a concerted and structured view as to what, when, where, how, why and to whom details are communicated? Putting careful consideration to this often under-estimated but critical consideration can determine if a plan fails or succeeds. It is easy to over-communicate too soon to the extent that an idea or an initiative gets shot down before it is given thoughtful consideration.

PEOPLE

Needless to say, people deliver results. Always pay full attention to your people. They truly are the biggest and most tangible asset that all managers in any business has.

Summary

In summary, if we always plan and make sure that a process is in place to implement our plans, we are starting out on the right road, and with a structured and deliberate pace of communications of plans, objectives and ideas we help ensure our people deliver the right results and bond them with a purpose of making profits and creating incremental shareholder value. A disciplined and deliberate application of the *Lincoln 6Ps* is powerfully cohesive, by making everyone involved feel like peas in a pod!

NOTES

THE MEN NORMALLY BOAST OF THE BIG PICTURE, BUT IT IS THE WOMEN WHO ENDURE AND DELIVER SUPERB AND DETAILED WORK!

Why women should see greater success than men in business

I t is yawningly obvious that men and women are truly different. But who makes the better entrepreneur? Obviously, this topic has the potential to be controversial and irk the sensibilities of both men and women. (Ladies, I am not treading the path of a male chauvinist here. Please bear with me. Patience is indeed a virtue!) So it would be prudent to understand the traits of successful entrepreneurs, who have built great companies, big and small... When you've had the great idea, developed a unique value proposition, established key differentiation from your competitors, secured the funds and the required skill sets, there is a unique set of behavioral and personality traits that will come to the fore...

1. **Interpersonal and verbal communication skills**
2. **A keen intuitive mindset**
3. **Good listening skills**
4. **Abstract reasoning**
5. **Peripheral vision**
6. **Sustainable mindset**
7. **Kaizen attitude**
8. **Multi-tasking capability**
9. **Independence, endurance and orientation to detail**

The art of entrepreneurship: must-have behavioral and personality traits

1 **Interpersonal and verbal communication skills** Business is all about people to people (P2P) connections, rather than B2C or B2B as it is commonly expressed. Most business is done among people who have built relationships over a period of time. Good communications and interpersonal relationships among all stakeholders including customers, employees, partners and shareholders and suppliers are essential to the success of any business.

2 **A keen intuitive mindset** In business, decisions about suppliers, partners and employees often have to be made on the fly. Small businesses do not have the luxury of time that large corporations have. A right or wrong decision could determine whether a business will survive or not. Having a keen intuitive sense is therefore essential for entrepreneurs.

3 **Good listening skills** This is different and separate from the required communications and interpersonal relationship traits already described. Good listening skills are always good to have, but for entrepreneurs this is a must. Often what is said and intended are not the same. Missing cues could mean false expectations and wasted time. This is not a luxury that entrepreneurs have. Knowing the differences between what is said and what is meant, and deciphering and acting on what was said, what was intended to be said and what you actually heard, is really a critical success factor for most entrepreneurs. Understanding the nuances of interpersonal communication is especially important in the current age of globalization and transmigration of cultures from different parts of the world.

4 **Abstract reasoning** Abstract or inductive reasoning is the ability to analyze information and solve problems in a complex, thought-based level. Entrepreneurs have to form hypotheses around their business ideas and processes, and be able to solve problems at a complex level. Business is not a linear logical application, but often requires complex and multi-faceted problem-solving capabilities. Entrepreneurship requires the ability to detect patterns, trends, and understand the relationships between verbal and non-verbal ideas.

5 **Peripheral vision** Small businesses and entrepreneurs do not have the budget for an army of research consultants to identify changes in customer needs, opportunities and threats. Often these market changes, opportunities and threats begin as weak signals from the periphery. Most companies large or small have not developed this capability in sufficient capacity. Successful entrepreneurs have an almost innate ability to see at the periphery where signals are weak at best.

6 **Sustainable mindset** Good entrepreneurship requires prudent and calculated risk taking. It is not about taking huge risks with other people's money. It is not just about building or creating something for the short term. It requires a long-term view, taking into account all stakeholder considerations. It includes knowledge and best practise sharing so that employees and other shareholders are well equipped to sustain their enthusiasm over the long haul.

7 **Kaizen attitude** The Japanese concept of 'kaizen' or continuous improvement is a must for successful entrepreneurship. It means not resting on your laurels or focusing on a single goal achievement. Good entrepreneurship requires people to be receptive to other's ideas. Good entrepreneurship also requires a balanced dosage of tempered self-appraisal and self-critical abilities.

8 **Multi-tasking capability** During the early stage of a business, entrepreneurs are often required to address multiple facets and aspects of their business. Due to the innate nature of small businesses and limited resource availability, good entrepreneurship requires this very important but often ignored capability.

9 **Endurance and detail orientation** Due to the limited resource capability of small businesses, good entrepreneurship requires that the entrepreneur be healthy and able to do monotonous tasks often enduring long and lonely periods. Most entrepreneurs are independent and able to be detail oriented and operational. Entrepreneurs can't survive with just the 'big picture' thinking capability alone.

Experts have discovered some real differences in the way that men and women's brains are structured and in the way we react to events and stimuli. So who makes the better entrepreneur, men or women? It is an established fact that women communicate more effectively than men. Young girls say their first words, learn to speak, read and are better in coping with language than boys. As adults, women are more fluent and have better command of languages. When a woman communicates with another human being, they look right into the other person's eyes and generally hold that eye contact longer than men. A woman's relationships are deeper and more sustainable than a man's. Her sensitivities to the externalities are more and deeper than a man's. (If you need further proof, look at the sexes of children in language remedial classes, or the ones that stutter.) Men have a pronounced need to fulfill their goals and women rank relationships with others first.

Speaking to a few men and women entrepreneurs and professionals to get their views on this subject, it was interesting to note that most men felt that men were better in business. Most women did not want to generalize or stereotype any one!

The best insight was provided by Georgie Hearson and Claire Fenner, co-founders of Heels and Deals, a Dubai-based network and consulting firm for women entrepreneurs.

'In our opinion women and men are equally good in business but they possess different strengths and weaknesses. For example, women are excellent at multi-tasking, enabling them to manage multiple business functions simultaneously, which in turn is a benefit to working mothers who not only run their own businesses but their homes", said Georgie Hearson.

Claire Fenner added "As we all know, women are excellent communicators whether it be through the spoken word or written word. If you get 200 women in a room speed networking the energy is phenomenal! The women know how to use this skill to their advantage!

"When it comes to supporting each other men are maybe more guarded and less likely to seek help from their colleagues or peers for fear of being seen as weak, whereas women are willing to look for help when required as well as support each other.

"In our opinion successful companies are those that work with the best in their field like we do at Heels & Deals."

Women have a superior and keener experience of all the senses, and better intuition. This relative observation of the heightened sensory perception of women is mainly due to the bluntness of the male senses. It is also known that women have a keener sense of nuances, intonation and meaning, and more easily pick up social cues and intensity of conversations and expressions.

Men are often utterly frustrated and exasperated at a woman's reaction to what they say. Women tend to be better judges of character. As we age, women have a better memory for names and faces, and a greater sensitivity to other people's preferences.

All this makes women more **intuitive** than men, but who is a better listener? Scientists have confirmed that sounds are more acute to a woman than a man. (During my early years of marriage to Carol, I often wondered why she kept insisting that I was yelling and that I needed to 'tone' down. I am enlightened now!) The combination of their deeper multi-sensory awareness and hearing skills makes women **better listeners**.

And who has better **abstract reasoning**? We have all heard that a man's brain is programmed for hunting. Men are laser focused and goes for the kill (rhetorically speaking). Women's brains can decipher a wider range of information. Women are equipped to receive a wider range of sensory information, to connect, correlate, compute, relate and act on that information with greater facility and agility. When entering a parking garage, men generally look and head to the direction of where their car is parked. Women on the other hand look around, notice faces (and strangers) and calculate possible threats perceived or otherwise. Men can definitely better grasp a situation as a whole and think globally. However, women think locally, relying on details and the nuances that matter. Women have a better capability of rewinding relevant information over and over.

Could this all be about women having better **peripheral vision**? Men have a firmer sense of direction. They need to track, trace and navigate the path to their goal. In other words, men see in a narrow field – mild tunnel vision – with greater concentration on depth. They have a better sense of perspective than women. Women, however, take in better the bigger picture – literally speaking. Not only do women have literally a wider peripheral vision but women can also more easily store, for short periods at least, more irrelevant and random information than men. Men can excel only when the information is organized in some coherent form, or has specific relevance to them. The combination of an acute sensory awareness, a literal view of the world through the receptor cone and rod cells in their retina, and their overall intuitiveness gives women an advantage in sensing signals that are almost always too weak for men to detect.

Women are by nature, nurturing, caring and giving. Men are builders whilst women pass on the most valuable information for the positive evolution of the next generation. This innate ability to unselfishly nurture and give, gives them an advantage in ensuring that all under their care get the needed information to sustain in the long run. In business, this gives women an advantage as the combination of their superior communications and personal relationship skills and this need to care and share will ensure that all shareholders are considered and the business focus is on the long-term **sustainability** of the enterprise.

Men are normally satisfied with their own performance. Women on the other hand are self-critical and often have a low self-appraisal of their work. Men are more independent in their thoughts and actions, whilst women seek out and are open to suggestions, comments, and opinions of others. It is important to be self critical and not satisfied with the status quo to strive for continuous improvement or **kaizen**.

We have all heard that women are superior at **multi-tasking**. Scientific studies have proven this. It should not be too surprising. Look at how working mothers do it. How they juggle a career, work, study, child care, cooking and home care all at the same time. Men should salute the women who do this, day in and day out.

As for independence, endurance and detail orientation, we know that women have longer life spans and are less prone to getting sick. Therefore in the macro sense, they are more enduring. Women also perform well when required to do monotonous and arduous tasks. Look around your company and the different projects being tasked and completed. Who amongst them works independently and looks into every detail. The men normally boast of the big picture, but it is the women who endure and deliver superb and detailed work!

NOTES

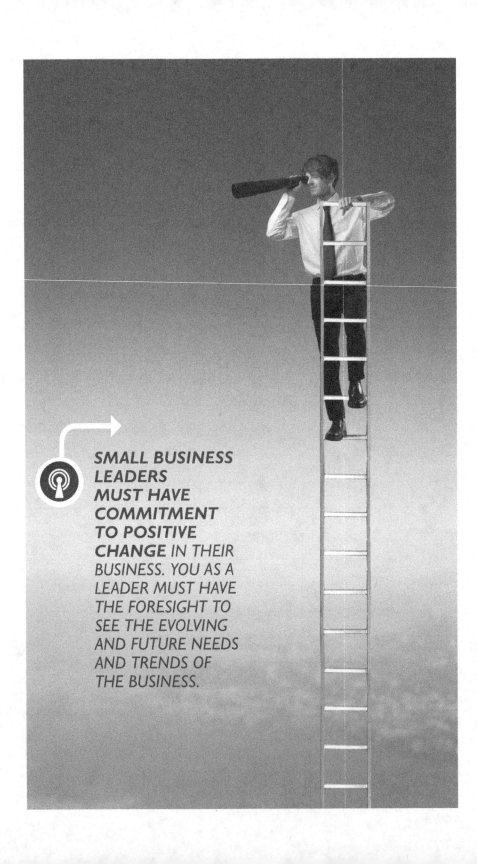

SMALL BUSINESS LEADERS MUST HAVE COMMITMENT TO POSITIVE CHANGE IN THEIR BUSINESS. YOU AS A LEADER MUST HAVE THE FORESIGHT TO SEE THE EVOLVING AND FUTURE NEEDS AND TRENDS OF THE BUSINESS.

LEADERSHIP MATTERS!

Definition, characteristics and components of a great business leader

I am often asked by many folks as to what leadership means for me. I have also often noticed that most small business owners and managers fail to see and internalize what leadership truly means. Unfortunately, there is not a single dimension or factor that you can attribute to someone's leadership capabilities. Enough has been written on leadership and leadership styles. There are many definitions. However, I have observed some common leadership traits by leaders of very successful small businesses. In essence, these leaders often determine the positive or negative outcomes for their businesses – whether their company sustains and grows and whether their customers or employees are happy and satisfied.

On a personal note, I am dedicating this chapter on leadership to the great small and large corporate leaders that I have had the pleasure of working with, observing and emulating them across my 30-plus years of management experience across different geographies and markets...

 A NOTE ON LEADERSHIP STYLES I have often heard the misnomer, "leadership style". Leadership is much more than style. It is a characteristic or quality that involves a totality of character, morality, motivation and many others.

So what are the dimensions, attributes and traits of a leader?

- **Conceptualize and visualize** – As a SME owner or manager, a leader is someone who can conceptualize and visualize a future for his or her business.

- **Leading people** – Small business owners must lead people to a greater outcome than it otherwise would have been. Period!

- **Steer and motivate** – A small business leader must have the ability to steer and motivate a group of people to a common purpose.

- **Empowerment** – To be a true leader, a small business owner or manager must empower others and believe that it is this empowerment that is the key to their success.

- **Confidence** – Small business leaders who have developed an idea or a business that has passed his or her "moral compass" test and one who has evaluated his or her risks will then must be committed to the vision, idea or project with deep rooted confidence that is conveyed to everyone around them.

- **Courage** – Leadership in small business also means having the courage to take corrective action to improve your business even if it means that you will have to fire a few employees.

- **Character** – As small business owners and leaders, you must demonstrate something that may be defined as "character". You must have the highest integrity of soul and purpose so that others are absolutely certain that whatever you, as the small business leader advocates, is what is best for the business.

- **Convince others** – In a SME setting, a leader is one who is able to convince others to join him/her on the journey. In small businesses, leaders must have the ability to share their vision, purpose and passion with others so that others are willing to do remarkable things – things that they didn't believe they could do.

- **Impetus for positive change** – Leadership in a small business also means making a difference, creating a positive change around you and facilitating the impetus that creates an atmosphere of change that improves the world, or at least the small part of the business world that you are in.

- **Change agent** – Small business owners and investors should be the change agents for changing things that can be changed, of providing new thinking, new energy, to an existing situation that needs to be changed or improved.

- **A sense of practical optimism** – It is said that great leaders are often optimistic. It is also said that pessimists make lousy leaders.

- **Exemplification of a set of behaviors** – In small businesses, leadership is exemplified by a set of series of behaviors. At the very core is the belief that things will get better. The small business leader will have to use his or her pulpit as the owner to influence others to help.

- **Work, emotion, and inspiration** – A small business leader must have an excellent work ethic, have a high emotional intelligence and is able to inspire others to join his or her journey.

- **Paced communications** – Small business owners should have the ability to pace and communicate effectively and share their vision widely across to all stakeholders. These effective communications will allow others to see, share and participate in their vision!

- **Always accept blame** – Small business leaders must be quick to accept the blame when blame occurs.

- **Sustained actions** – A small business leader must demonstrate leadership by sustained actions over a period time.

- **Sense of practicality and realism** – SME owners and managers must be practical and It means facing the reality of business, and not have pie-in-the-sky dreams and, conversely, not being overly pessimistic.

- **Decisive and deliberate** – It means that small business owners must take the bull by the horn and deal with situations. It means connecting the dots in business and life. Leadership for small business also means taking concrete actions in your business and biting the bullet when you have to.

- **Listen, translate, decide and motivate** – Small business owners must have the ability to listen, translate, decide and motivate others.

- **Source of guidance** – A small business owner or manager must often be the authority sought out for information, guidance and consultation.

- **Respected** – It goes without saying that a small business owner or manager must be respected by all stakeholders...

- **Foresight and evolutionary** – Small business leaders must have commitment to positive change in their business. You as a leader must have the foresight to see the evolving and future needs and trends of the business.

- **Doing what is right** – A small business owner or manager must do what is right for the business. It certainly is not an effort for recognition, glory and receipt of accolades.

- **Perceptive** – Small business owners must be perceptive about people, issues, challenges and trends around them.

- **Strong willed** – Small business leaders must possess strong will that what they believe is best is, indeed, best.

- **Create a buzz or energy around them** – Small business owners must have the ability to create energy, motivation and action in a group of people based on your business' mutual values and ideas.

- **Intellectual** – Small business owners and managers must exhibit Intellectual leadership by taking risks with ideas and by challenging existing belief systems and urging your employees to react, think, argue, and grow as depicted through your everyday communications to their employees.

What is the true nutshell when it comes to leadership?

I think true leadership is demonstrated by example; in addition, it is the creation and support of a structure that allows all members to contribute to the best of their ability.

Further, my definition of leadership is that it is an opportunity for a person to assume a role in which they can interact with colleagues to achieve a certain end or goal. Leadership is the quality required of a leader to make that interaction occur in a meaningful way.

All the above dimensions, characteristics, attribute and behaviors could be summarized into 3 main categories or components. These are the 3 leadership components that matter. Each of these components is important. The weightage of each of this component depends on the SME owner or manager's role and level in an organization.

Small business owners and SME investors and managers can apply the S.O.P principles outlined in this chapter to determine the level of importance and weighting that they should give to each of the leadership components.

Component 1 – A leader must be strategic The first part about being a leader is being Strategic. You really need to have the big picture and know the trends, the competitive aspects of your industry and all that good stuff that folks learn in school and in everyday life. You need to have a view as to where your industry is heading, the new technologies, the substitutes and so forth.

Component 2 – A leader must have operational management knowhow and capability Knowing the big picture alone is not good. You need to have an **Operational** know how of your business and your industry in general. You need to be able to roll up your sleeves and get your hands dirty in the muddle and puddle of business. Most small business owners do this.

Component 3 – People leadership matters Last but not least, your **People** leadership is very important. It is the people in your business who are delivering the results for which we are all paid for or are making money through their efforts.

A caveat on the three components

It should be remembered that as one moves up the corporate ladder or when a business grows, and when responsibility increases (hopefully with your pay and perks along with it), the right dosage or rather the right weightage of the strategy, operations and people leadership skill components are required.

For example, a CEO of an established and growing small business will have to have the highest weightage on his strategic skills, know-how and application. A general manager in your business, who manages a large number of people, would probably require a heavy weightage on his or her operational and people leadership skills. A small business owner just about starting his or her business will probably require equal application of each of the strategy, operational and people leadership components.

So remember: leadership is not about being a great strategist, or knowing and doing the nuts and bolts of your business or about just being a good people manager. It is about having the right combination of all the three at the right phase of your career or business life that matters. Having the big picture or being a micro manager or being a good people manager alone is not going to get you to achieve your dreams. You need the right combination of all the three.

Summary

A FINAL NOTE ON LEADERSHIP – don't confuse leadership with management. As one of my favorite management gurus once said "Management is doing things right; leadership is doing the right things".

In summary, as a small business owner, achieving the strategic, operational and people leadership skills alone are not enough. Small business owners MUST have the quality of leadership and the capability to influence the behavior of others to an intended direction. As a small business owner or manager, you may influence by rhetoric, logic, action and/or personal example. In the end, it all boils down to "We should do this; follow me."

In other words, knowledge, wealth, position or power has nothing to do with leadership. Simply put, a leader is one who leads or guides!

As Dwight Eisenhower said "Leadership is the art of getting someone else to do something you want done because he wants to do it".

NOTES

PRIMA DONNAS WHO MAKE OUT THAT THE BUSINESS IS DEPENDENT SOLELY ON THEM NEED CAREFUL MANAGEMENT. COMMUNICATE CLEARLY THAT NO ONE IS INDISPENSABLE.

BIG PICTURE
MANAGEMENT

Successfully connecting the business to customers and profits

As children, we would all have drawn 'connect the dots' pictures. They are still often given out in family restaurants to ensure that kids are occupied and are not bored, whilst they are waiting for their food to arrive. In this game, the player is required to connect the numbers which appear to be distributed randomly on a sheet of paper. Once the numbers are all fully connected, those random dots will reveal an image or picture of something.

Business and life itself is made up of a series of dots that often appear discrete, disparate and disconnected. Very often, instances, cues, actions, suggestions, choices, decisions and others all appear to be so unconnected. But despite the seemingly inconsequential and illusory image it gives, there are significant consequences to each of the choices that we make in business. When a series of actions, words and deeds are connected, they give us a truer picture of our business reality – just as if we were connecting the dots to better visualize a business scenario.

A long time ago, in a distant country, a small business hotel owner was seeking to hire a general manager to run his business. The key qualities needed? Experience in the hospitality industry, good people and communications skills, and the ability to develop and drive new and incremental business to the hotel. There were many candidates to choose from.

There was one particular candidate that stood out from the rest. This candidate had more years of verifiable experience and was a proven high performer. The only problem was that the stronger candidate was not of the owner's preferred ethnic origin. The owner was in a dilemma. He had another candidate that did not have the same number of years of experience and his entire experience was not verifiable. This other contending candidate (albeit the weaker one) was the same as the small business owner's ethnicity.

Most folks are comfortable with people having different cultural and social backgrounds. And there are, of course, laws now in place in most countries that ensure that discrimination based on race, creed or gender is outlawed and illegal.

This small business owner called me for my advice. He had a personal dilemma. He felt more comfortable hiring his 'own kind' despite admitting the other candidate was far superior than the candidate who had the same ethnicity as the owner.

Just think about the irony of this situation. Here is a man who had invested a considerable amount of his own money, time and effort building a business. This man, who took such a business risk in investing in this hotel, was letting his personal feelings and emotions blur his decision making.

For me, the decision was obvious. I encouraged him to go back to his original objective, as to why he wanted to hire a general manager for his hotel. I further requested him to answer honestly, as to who can deliver his growth ambitions. I asked him to '**connect the dots**', as to why he would or would not hire any one of the other candidates. The owner did the right thing and he hired the stronger candidate.

If the hiring judgment of an individual business owner can be so clouded in this way, then what does it tell us about all the businesses that have institutional investors run by managers who have neither risks nor personal equity invested in their operation?

The next time we hire or make an offer to a prospective candidate, we need ensure that we connect the dots! Do not judge the person based on looks, colour, accent, sex, height, weight or the colour of their hair.

Go back to your objectives and connect the dots! If these objectives call for a 'green, short, fat, one eyed jack' then, so be it! Do everything possible to meet the stated objectives and do not blur decisions with non relevant emotions and issues.

Failure to connect the dots in this way, can be to the serious detriment of the business and it is a phenomenon that is more common than people realize. As these few examples illustrated, we need be prudent and economical at all times, but we also need reflect upon whether an action or a decision is optimal, and whether it is in the best interest of the business to make decisions that are unconnected.

2 Hiring too few (or excessively cheap labor) customer-facing staff One of the biggest mistakes a company can make is to have too few people dedicated to serving customers. To add to this conundrum, is the expectation that those employees who are in place should work extra hard to cope with that deficiency. Unhappy employees mean unhappy customers. Those unhappy customers will not come back to buy more. Unhappy customers will tell other potential customers of their dissatisfaction. Meanwhile, unhappy employees will leave the business, taking with them all their experience and the training investments made in them by the business.

OVER TIME THE BUSINESS WILL BLEED ITS PROFESSIONAL COMPETENCY, because every company's core competency (especially in a service business) is derived from the experience and professionalism of its employees.

2 Location! Location! Location! Why do so many small business owners establish their businesses far away from the main business district in which they operate, just to save money on rental? Getting an optimal location with the lowest rental possible is the right thing to do. Getting into a location just because it is the cheapest, is not the answer. Customers, employees and business associates need access to the business and it has to be conveniently located. If they cannot, they will exit at the earliest opportunity and take with them potential business opportunities.

3 Not treating employees with respect and as professionals It is too easy for business managers and owners to treat their employees as task workers and, at times, with disrespect and disdain. People respond best to empathy, kindness and respect. As employees, they will usually give much more that what is expected of them. They do not need reminding who is boss. This does not mean that they do not need to be coaxed when they slacken in their performance, but as a rule of thumb when employees are respected and treated professionally, they will in turn treat customers with respect as professionals.

4 **Not creating an environment conducive to employee contribution and productivity** Too many business managers and owners are unnecessarily paranoid and secretive of their business development activities. (While it can be beneficial to be slightly paranoid about your competition, this should not be extended to your own employees!) Employees respond best to trust and trusted employees want and can contribute significantly to the growth of the business they are working in.

5 **Not getting rid of poor-performing employees** The odds are high that there will always be one or two employees who do not perform as well as they need to and the advice must be to get rid of the non performer. He or she might be even your spouse's kith and kin, but they need to be removed as the costs incurred employing them are three-fold: From the onset, the business is paying some one for under performing. Secondly, the business is bearing the opportunity cost of not getting incremental revenue from a potential new employee who could be brought in to replace a non performer. Thirdly, the business is bearing the opportunity cost of other employees having to chip in to cover for a non performer, thereby reducing their contribution.

6 **Not firing a prima donna or a disruptive employee** Similarly, disruptive employees and prima donnas who make out that the business is dependent solely on them, need careful management. Communicate clearly that no one is indispensable. As a famous CEO of one of the largest telecommunication companies in the world once said "We don't need a team of stars. We need a star team". Prima donnas and disruptive employees can slowly suck the air out of everyone around them. They affect employee productivity and morale.

7 **Limiting your marketing investments to save money** Many small business firms try to save money on their marketing spend by budgeting for only very limited or no promotional activities at all. It is not enough to promote a business by just releasing a press release, or participating in some exhibition or event, or blasting social media messages to an untargeted audience. In fact, this can be counter-productive. Investment in promotional activities is needed to create awareness, before a proposition becomes relevant

to the target customer base. Connect the dots and think about this. For the proposition to be relevant, it has to work and considered to be functional by the target market. Rule number one then, is not to take short cuts in the design of the proposition. Rule number two: segment the market and target it appropriately. Blasting a communications campaign to all and sundry is just a sheer waste of money and can be counter-productive to your brand image, as most people are annoyed at being slammed with junk mail. A business wins customer loyalty and repeat business only once its target market is aware that you exist and once they know that the functionality of the proposition works. Your target market has to connect emotionally to your proposition. Keep in mind that the emotional relevance of your proposition only occurs when the experience works or if it is truly functional. Only then can a business think of repeat business. In other words, the business will not grow without sufficient investment in the brand.

TAKING SHORT CUTS only limits a company's growth potential and might even not sustain it in the long run.

8 **Saving money by limiting channel incentives**
Why would a growing company want to limit the pay outs made to its high-performing sales employees? In one case, sales employee incentives were capped at 110% of their expected target delivery. In most companies, 80% of incremental new sales come from about 20% of the sales folks. These are professionals who are driven by their need to be the top earners. But here most of them kept their new prospects close to their chest, as they were limited to the 110% achievement target. Just imagine the potential if this compensation target was designed around 200% or 300% cap on their variable pay. Why even limit the incentives achieved over and above given targets? A business is only limiting its own growth with this artificial ceiling, based upon some purported belief that top sales performers are not necessarily motivated by their incentives!

There are many other examples of scenarios where managers fail to connect the dots:

- **Not putting in place structures,** processes and people with clear empowerment, responsibilities and accountabilities.

- **Giving limited** or no empowerment to key employees.

- **Investing in excessively large numbers of people** for non-core and administrative support services.

- **Making inadequate investments in information technology** and telecommunication systems.

- **Keeping prices artificially high,** based on fallacious advise from accountants, who do not necessarily have a cross-functional view of the business.

- **Setting unrealistic margin expectations** and expecting higher levels of commitment from customers year on year.

The ability to reflect on an action or decision to consider the implications of that action or decision is a most critical aspect of business management, and something that is achieved by 'connecting the dots'. So remember that just because you keep doing something, over and over, it might not always be the right thing.

Conversely, just because you are not doing something may not necessarily mean you are doing it because it is the wrong thing. It could just mean that you have not connected the dots! As Mahatma Gandhi once said, "An error does not become truth by reason of multiplied propagation, nor does truth become error because nobody sees it".

NOTES

FOR SMALL BUSINESS OWNERS, *A LACK OF UNDERSTANDING OF THE VIRTUOUS-VICIOUS CYCLE CONCEPT COULD LEAD TO A RAPID DEMISE OF THE BUSINESS.*

THE POWER OF VIRTUOUS AND VICIOUS CYCLES IN BUSINESS

How to accentuate your virtuous cycles and disrupt your vicious cycles

Life, as you know, is a cycle: everything you do or don't do comes round. So have you heard about the proven concept of virtuous and vicious cycles? Let's say you have. But have you really given much thought as to how it affects your personal life, career or business? The concepts of virtuous and vicious cycles are critically important for any business, whatever the size, scope or industry. For small business owners and SME investors, a lack of understanding of this concept could mean sickness or even a quick death of their business.

I have often noted in my discussions with small business owners and/or investors, their utter lack of understanding of these concepts and am saddened to see how they are putting their business at risk or how they themselves are limiting the growth of their business, through misinformation or lack of understanding. In fact, even large companies, governments, politicians and others make the classic mistake of not accentuating a virtuous cycle or not disrupting a vicious cycle to their own detriment. All it takes are identifying the key areas and taking a few common sense-based steps. Once you take these steps you will find an immediate difference to your bottom line, no matter how hopeless the business situation may have seemed earlier.

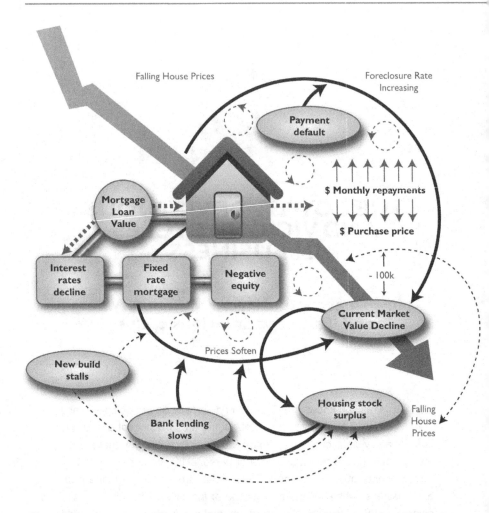

Falling House Prices

Foreclosure Rate
Increasing

Payment
default

$ Monthly repayments

$ Purchase price

Mortgage
Loan
Value

- 100k

Interest
rates
decline

Fixed
rate
mortgage

Negative
equity

Current Market
Value Decline

Prices Soften

New build
stalls

Housing stock
surplus

Falling
House
Prices

Bank lending
slows

Figure 29:
Example of a
vicious cycle in
action.

The concept of virtuous and vicious cycles can have a critical impact on business. These describe a set of controlled or uncontrolled events that reiterate or reinforce themselves through a feedback loop. A virtuous cycle accentuates and enhances the outcome, while a vicious cycle diminishes or often destroys the outcome. Both cycles have positive or negative feedback loops, in which each reiteration of the cycle reinforces the first outcome. These cycles will continue in their positive (virtuous) or negative (vicious) direction and will build up to a critical mass until it is disrupted by forces or factors that diminishes or reduces the negative or positive outcomes until finally the cycle is broken.

Classic gains of virtuous business cycles

For small business owners and SME investors. in particular, a lack of understanding of this concept could lead to a rapid demise of the business. Without a full appreciation of its power, business executives are putting themselves and their business at risk and are limiting the growth of their business. To their own detriment, many large companies, governments, politicians

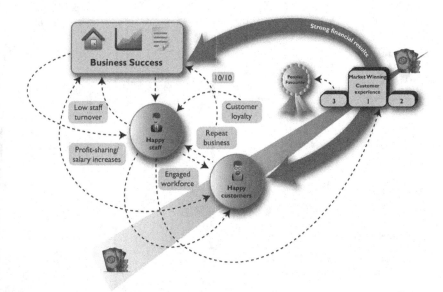

and others make the classic mistake of not accentuating a virtuous cycle and/or not disrupting a vicious cycle. [We should ponder a scenario. If Lehman Brothers had been saved, and its toxic subprime assets had been assumed through some US Government guarantees, then would the commercial banks that offer credit to fund large and small businesses have taken the drastic steps to freeze commercial paper (short term borrowings of companies)?

This freezing by the commercial banks resulted in many companies not having sufficient cash flows to fund the capital and operating expenditures required to keep their business afloat. This resulted in many folks being laid off, which in turn eroded public confidence further, which dried up demand,

Figure 30: Example of a virtuous cycle in operation.

Figure 31: An extreme example of a hiring vicious cycle.

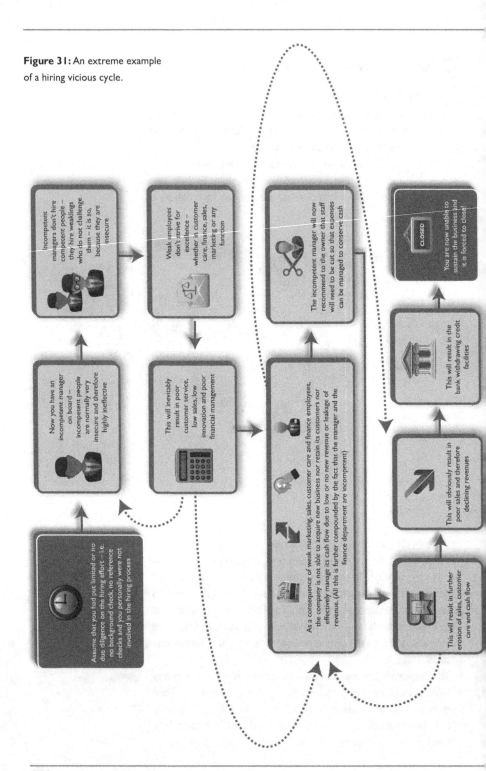

Incompetent managers don't hire competent people – they hire weaklings who do not challenge them – it is so, because they are insecure

Weak employees don't strive for excellence – whether in customer care, finance, sales, marketing or any function

The incompetent manager will now recommend to the owner that staff will need to be cut so that expenses can be managed to conserve cash

CLOSED

You are now unable to sustain the business and it is forced to close!

Now you have an incompetent manager on board – incompetent people are normally very insecure and therefore highly ineffective

This will inevitably result in poor customer service, low sales, low innovation and poor financial management

As a consequence of weak marketing, sales, customer care and finance employees, the company is not able to acquire new business nor retain its customers nor effectively manage its cash flow due to low or no new revenue or leakage of revenue. (All this is further compounded by the fact that the manager and the finance department are incompetent)

This will result in the bank withdrawing credit facilities

This will obviously result in poor sales and therefore declining revenues

Assume that you had put limited or no due diligence on the hiring effort – i.e. no background check, no reference checks and you personally were not involved in the hiring process

This will result in further erosion of sales, customer care and cash flow further exacerbating the economic environment!] So it is vitally important that we appreciate how to intervene to accentuate virtuous cycles in ways that help achieve some business breakthrough – and how to disrupt a vicious cycle to defuse its detrimental consequences.

Examples of virtuous and vicious cycles that can affect your business

The best way to demonstrate the impact of virtuous and vicious cycles is through actual examples:

Scenario 1- Hiring and firing

Imagine that your business is expanding and that you need to hire a manager for your business. Assume that you had put limited or no due diligence on the hiring effort – i.e. no background check, no reference checks and you personally were not involved in the hiring process. Now you have an incompetent manager on board. In the main, incompetent people can be insecure and therefore highly ineffective. Experience shows that incompetent managers don't hire competent people – they hire weaklings who do not challenge them – it is so, because they are insecure. Weak employees don't strive for excellence – whether in customer care, finance, sales, marketing or any function. This will inevitably result in poor customer service, low sales, low innovation and poor financial management.

As a consequence of weak marketing, sales, customer care and finance employees, the company will not be able to acquire new business, nor retain its customers, nor effectively manage its cash flow due to low or no new revenue (or leakage of revenue).

All this is further compounded by the fact that the manager and the finance department are incompetent. The incompetent manager will now recommend to the owner that staff will need to be cut so that expenses can be managed to conserve cash. This will result in further erosion of sales, customer care and cash flow. It will obviously result in poor sales and therefore declining revenues, possibly lead to the bank withdrawing credit facilities. You are now unable to sustain the business and it is forced to close!

As evident from this example, a simple act like not putting enough due diligence on hiring key employees ultimately could bring a business down. What would you have done? How would you disrupt this vicious cycle?

Look around many businesses and it soon becomes apparent that this is not fiction: the wrong people get hired because someone liked their looks, ethnicity or that they came in cheap. Imagine the opportunity cost put on the table by these stupid and short-sighted decisions! Imagine how de-motivated the good, high-performing employees must be, watching an incompetent getting paid more than them while they slowly destroy the business.

Scenario 2 – Costing and Pricing

Imagine a restaurant offering a menu that can entice the gastronomical exigencies of any passing customer. It is vital that the menu is priced correctly. It has to be competitive: there are many well known restaurants in the area. The incompetent company accountant (perhaps the same person from the previous scenario) advises you that the menu has to be priced to produce a margin of X% based on some idiotic fully-allocated costs and volume of sales based on current trading levels, inappropriately allocated across all the fine cuisine and drinks that are listed on the menu. Costing is done by the incompetent accountant, based on fully-allocated method and current volumes and not one based on variable costs, or one priced to drive increased sales.

Marketing leverage to set pricing correctly is diminished due to these fallacious cost assumptions. Marketing is unable to address perceived value of the service and food proposition to its customers. Due to low volume assumptions and the need to generate a reasonable margin, price is set relatively high. Marketing is neither assertive nor competent enough to challenge the finance teams' assumptions. Customer demand decreases. Price is again reset, based on decreased demand and more fallacious assumptions. Revenues and customers are in decline. Good employees leave due to their inability to generate enough tips. The management is advised by the accountant to curb costs and put in excess control due to the decreased demand. The restaurant buys cheaper quality raw materials and downgrades or downsizes critical customer facing and kitchen employees. Service deteriorates, sales dwindle to a halt. Revenue drops and the restaurant is hardly able to survive. The rest is history!

Scenario 3 – Customer Service and Sales Targeting

Imagine you are a distributor of office equipment in the region who has recently won the sole distributorship rights in a country for a major well known Original Equipment Manufacturer (OEM). You won this right for sole distributorship due to your excellent sales record. You have just been given a new sales and revenue target by your principal (the OEM). Your goal is to reach a certain sales target in the current fiscal year.

The company hires additional sales people – an operation that went well due to experience of having successfully done it in the past, and sales increase. The customer service team is under a heavy burden to service the increasing demands, however – these problems are not apparent to you, due to focus on driving increased sales.

Some past loyal customers begin to complain of poor service. The company is not unduly worried as it is bringing in a lot of new customers. The unsatisfied customers start to desert the business. Your sales folks are burdened with calls for support from your dissatisfied customers, as they are not getting the requisite service from your customer service and after-sales service departments. Your sales folks respond positively – they are excellent sales folks that will not ignore their customer requests. The sales team is not able to meet their targets as they are spending a lot of their productive time on after-sales service issues. The company's top performers leave the company due to their disillusionment of the management's lack of focus on service, resulting in them losing their income.

Sales deteriorate. The company imposes cuts – non-sales folks are impacted the most. Customer service deteriorates further and customer churn increases. Sales continue to drop as your remaining sales folks are unable to focus on bringing in the incremental new sales but are rather compelled to attend to customer service issues. Your principal withdraws your sole distributorship rights. Your competitors smell blood! You are history!

Understanding the true power of V cycles

Many a times, small business owners and investors ignore to their own detriment issues that are not bringing immediate incremental sales or cash flow. How would you have disrupted the feedback loops that were destroying these companies?

The point to the three examples are that management time, attention and dedication is needed across the business – from hiring, to investing in new propositions to extend your product life cycle, and spending on customer service and marketing. These all will determine whether the business is able to sustain, prosper and win. Do not be fooled by the tunnel vision of bean counters.

Pay attention and disrupt your vicious cycles whilst accentuating the positive feedback loops. You will need courage, vision and understanding to take your business to the next level. Life is unpredictable but it really is in your power to disrupt any reinforcing feedback loop, positively or negatively.

BY BEING AWARE OF THE POTENTIAL UPSIDE AND DOWNSIDE of virtuous and vicious cycles, it definitely can make a difference on how we conduct our personal, professional or entrepreneurial life – know it, sense it and act upon it... a virtuous circle can eventually transform into a vicious circle if negative feedback is ignored!

NOTES

FACTORS THAT AFFECT BUSINESS VALUATION INCLUDE PROFITABILITY AND GROWTH POTENTIAL, THE UNIQUENESS OF THE VALUE PROPOSITION AND THE EXISTING PROVABLE CUSTOMER BASE.

HOW MUCH IS YOUR BUSINESS WORTH?

Learning simple financial formulas and applying them to know the value of your business

O wners, investors and stakeholders of privately held companies need to know what their business is worth. Valuation is required not just when selling a business; it is needed to better understand how to develop appropriate strategies and tactics that will maximize the variables that drive business value. There are, in fact, many instances when a valuation exercise is required to establish the value of a company:

- An investor or entrepreneur may decide to invest or buy into a business, rather than starting one from scratch.
- An owner needs to establish the value of the company in order to contribute the appropriate number of shares to an Employee Stock Ownership Plan (ESOP).
- A value is needed to establish the percentage of ownership that any new investor receives in the company.
- An existing partner or partners may want to buy out the other partner's interests in a company.
- An owner might want to exit the business, change direction or possibly retire.

There are all sorts of accounting and financial formulas that can be applied here and expert opinion to be sought, but to provide insight and context we will explore this important theme in a way that should be understandable to any one running a small or medium-sized business.

Significant factors that affect the valuation of a business

Valuations reveal what the market thinks of a company, its management and strategy, its financial position and its prospects. There are many factors that affect the valuation of a business. They include the obvious ones like profitability and growth potential, the uniqueness of the value proposition of the business and the existing provable customer base. Other factors that are often not that obvious include tax credits for past losses, goodwill based on a company's reputation in the market, and proprietary processes and methods and/or patents awarded or pending that are not known or easily replicated.

Aspects like whether the business is in a defensive or growth phase in its market, sector drivers such as manufacturing costs, production volumes and sales prices and the impact these have on cash flow, also need to be taken into account.

For start-ups that have not generated any revenue and those that are still in the development stage, a key consideration includes the stage of development of technology. Valuations of start-ups vary significantly when a prototype is in development stage to a beta testing phase, to a stage when customers are actually willing to pay and use a product or service.

This noted, every business valuation follows some basic principles:

1 **Every business is valued based on its growth potential.** Growth is fundamental for any business. Without the potential for growth, there is really no reason for anyone to invest in or buy a business.

2 **Business investment capital comes from two sources.** Investment capital comes from investors investing money in the business and from borrowings. Therefore there is a cost of capital to consider – one is the opportunity cost of returns forgone from other investments, and the other is the actual cost of borrowing.

3 **Profits provide the only real returns.** The profits generated from a company can be reinvested to grow the business, used to pay off debts, or used to reward the business owners, investors and stakeholders with dividends. These parties and/or the potential buyers of the business can invest

their money somewhere else or in the stock market and can expect some reasonable returns, so the profitability or future profitability is the single biggest factor of any business.

4 **There is a time value of money.** A $100,000 sum paid at end of 5 years is not the same as if it is paid today, because some safe investments in the market or depositing the money in a bank, would produce some level of reasonable returns.

5 **Cash is king.** For almost all public companies, less than 10% of their market capitalization can be explained from the expected cash flows generated during a known planning period of say, five years. Trying to predict anything beyond a five-year business planning horizon has too many uncertainties. Analysts use the growth factor to forecast the terminal value or the continuing value of the business. This terminal value or continuing value accounts for about 95% of a company's market capitalization.

Valuation methods

1. ASSET-BASED VALUATION

This is done by estimating the value of the company's assets, but as assets are used to generate revenues this often under-estimates a growing business. Conversely, if a business has a large asset base but does not generate much cash, then its valuation would be lower than other more cash-generative companies.

There are three well-known asset-based valuation methods:

- **Modified book value technique** – This method adjusts the company's assets by looking at the historical value of the assets and adjusting this value to reflect current market values.
- **Replacement value technique** – The value of a company's assets are adjusted by deducting the cost it takes to replace or replenish the assets.
- **Liquidation value technique** – This is usually used in a forced-sale situation and assessed as if the company has ceased operations and its assets are to be liquidated and sold.

2. MARKET COMPARABLE VALUATION

This is difficult as no one business is exactly the same. The intrinsic value of a business can only be understood by going beyond just comparing valuations of other comparable businesses in the same industry sector. In this method, the value of comparable companies sold is divided by the earnings of those companies to derive a multiple which can be used to determine value. In this valuation technique, a company's current earnings are multiplied by the multiple factor to determine the value. It goes without saying that the higher the growth potential or lower the implicit and explicit risks, the higher the multiple and therefore the higher the valuation. In addition, a lot of ambiguous factors like a company's vulnerability to market and economic risks (lower multiple), the over dependency on a few key people for the success of the business (lower multiple) and other factors actually determine the multiples.

Goodwill factors like a company's reputation, unique location or customer relationships are often misrepresented when determining valuations using this method. The most common methods of doing market comparable valuation include:

- **Earnings multiple ratio method** – A company value is determined by multiplying the earnings to a multiple that is compared to the sale of other similar businesses.
- **Normalized earnings method** – This is similar to the earnings multiple method but it adjusts the earnings for 'unusual' items like the owner's salary or normalizing the earnings impact for extraordinary events that affected the earnings, like natural disasters or fires and others.

3. CASH FLOW-BASED VALUATION

This is one of the most commonly accepted methods of valuation as it takes into account the value by determining the cash-flow streams of the company and its growth potential. In simplistic terms, the Free Cash Flow (FCF) – which is the amount of cash generated by the business less the operating and capital expenditures and other reinvestments made – and the growth potential of the cash flow are both estimated. These cash flows are then discounted in today's value by using a required rate of return which takes into account the opportunity cost of money if it is invested in other investments, as well as the borrowing costs. The tax benefits for the interest paid on borrowings are also taken into account.

> *Earnings can be pliable as putty when a charlatan heads the company reporting them*
>
> Warren Buffet,
> investor

 1. Be sure of your motives of valuation beyond a windfall exit.

 2. There is no single best method to determine a business' worth, so compute the value using different methods and choose the best one.

 3. Both the buyer and the seller must be satisfied with the valuation.

 4. Both the buyer and seller should have access to business records.

 5. Valuations should be based on facts, not fiction.

 6. Both parties should deal with one another honestly and in good faith.

 7. Set realistic and conservative expectations and know your cut off value points (whether you are a buyer or seller) so that you would be very clear in your mind, when a firm offer comes through. A business is only worth how much someone is willing to pay for it.

 8. Get expert opinion (although it is you who will need to decide in the end!).

 9. Have a crystal clear view of the value blocks (both positive value enhancers and the negative potential value destroyers of your business valuation).

 10. Create multiple scenarios of the valuation model.

As Warren Buffet, the Sage of Omaha, and famous American entrepreneur, suggests, it is important that business owners and investors think seriously about their accounting practises and methods if they have plans to sell their interests in a business.

Figure 32: Ten golden rules of business valuation.

- Make sure that the financial records are impeccable, well managed, traceable and audited by reputable firms.

- Get experts to advise and help: Do not underestimate the value you might have to forgo if you do not have proper and auditable records.

- Ensure that business growth is sustainable and explore new ways to continue on a growth path.

NOTES

_____

_____

_____

_____

_____

_____

_____

_____

_____

_____

_____

_____

_____

_____

_____

_____

_____

_____

_____

_____

_____

I HAD A BUSINESS PLAN AND WAS ABLE TO RAISE MORE THAN $3 MILLION IN FUNDING FROM INDIVIDUAL INVESTORS. MY PARTNERS AND THE MAJORITY OF THE TOP MANAGEMENT TEAM THAT I HIRED WERE DEDICATED AND SUPERBLY COMPETENT INDIVIDUALS.

7TH HEAVEN – SUSTAINING AND GROWING YOUR BUSINESS

Valuable personal lessons learnt from a spectacular mistake

It was a typical San Francisco Bay morning, cool, bright and sunny, that day in the spring of 1999. I was on a yacht at the Half Moon Bay yacht club with my business partner John Thiele. With us was Dinesh Khurana, my other co-founder and business partner.

As fellow founders of my e-learning start up, we were discussing our equity structure, preferred shareholder rights, stock option plan, our employees and the potential management team we could get on board. We were also discussing at length the implications of the proposed commercial model, and were gleefully contemplating an IPO exit strategy.

As I look back, I am stupendously flabbergasted by the audacity of my idea. I had just resigned from my well-paying expatriate job in Tokyo, Japan. With my resignation went my very generous salary, bonuses and stock options. My wife Carol had to adjust back to life in the Bay area. On top of that, she was expecting our third child who was conceived in Tokyo. I had to buy a house and two cars at the same time – one for my family's use and the other for mine. We also had to settle our kids back to school in the United States. Yes, on top of all this, I was crazy enough to invest over $600,000 in cash and kind into a business to be launched in Osaka, Japan.

As I think about this last chapter, I can't but help remember the dots that I then spectacularly failed to connect. Yes indeed, my partners and I had a purposeful exit strategy. But come to think of it now, it was a pie-in-the sky dream.

The dots that I did not connect!

Flat rate and high speed internet access was nascent in Japan at that time. This was a pre-requisite to ensuring that my customers could enjoy unfettered online access.

On top of that we had developed 150 lessons for the Japanese market. Hindsight is certainly 20/20. I should have just developed about five or 10 lessons and gone after the B2B market versus trying to build a consumer brand with the paltry start -up capital that I had.

Instead of spending all our funds developing those lessons, I should have hired two or three competent sales account managers to target the human resources function in large companies. Had I done that, I would, in all probability, have sustained and grown the business.

I again failed to connect the dots as I should not have hired that many teachers to handle the calls from students in my call center. I had miserably failed in my forecasting and planning – and therefore, in my cash management.

I certainly should not have hired one useless Chief Technology Officer who personally contributed to about eight months of delay to my launch plan. This particular person was competent in his function. He absolutely had no idea on how to manage a team. The infighting and back stabbing in his team was unbelievable. I should have hired his replacement, Kristina Sterling, much sooner.

Further, I should not have hired all the artists and Flash programmers, but rather brought them on as contractors on a variable scheme. I should have fired at least two of my top management team who were just sucking up my bandwidth with their incompetency.

I should have stayed focused on the core basis of the business model, developing the e-learning content, rather than trying to create a world-famous learning portal with games, exam preparation classes and auction and others.

In hindsight, I should probably have not gone and entered into contracts with incompetent and unscrupulous vendors and offshore partners who kept changing my cost model.

Last but not least, I personally should have stayed away from the business once the funding and management team was in place. As the single largest investor, I let my ego and emotions overcome the better of me!

> " As the single largest investor, I let my ego and emotions overcome the better of me! "
>
> *John Lincoln,*
> *author*

The dots that I connected well

However, I did connect some dots well. I had a business plan and was able to raise more than $3 million in funding from individual investors. My partners and the majority of the top management team that I hired were dedicated and superbly competent individuals.

We had proper administration, accounting and legal contracts. This is not a trivial issue, as when we decided to shut the company, we paid off all the preferred shareholders $0.13 on the dollar for their investments. We renegotiated with all our creditors and probably paid about $0.20 to the dollar on moneys owed to them.

As common stock holders, my two partners, John and Dinesh, and I did not get a single cent back. On top of that, John and I had forgone our entire salaries for stock options that were worthless. But in the end, we were able to walk out of it cleanly.

We filed all the necessary papers and kept our records for 10 years (although California law only required us to keep records for seven years). We retrenched our employees in Osaka, Japan and in Foster City California. This was all done legally.

You see, when I had this great idea for the business, nothing could have stopped me from jumping into this bubbling frying pan. Despite my international experience of being a successful commercial manager and marketer, someone who had even been a protagonist in a major business school case study, I made colossal mistakes. I certainly hadn't connected all the dots. In hindsight, I wish I had.

This entrepreneurial experience taught me many valuable lessons on human frailties, market, completion, branding, commercial models, equity structuring and others.

So how do you reach nirvana on sustaining and growing your business? Is the profit bliss achievable? What are the dots that an entrepreneur or a SME owner or investor must connect before venturing into the perilous world of entrepreneurship? How do you reach that beatific "seventh heaven"?

Despite my international experience of being a successful commercial manager and marketer, I made colossal mistakes."

John Lincoln, author

The ultimate guide

There are many dots that you will have to connect to sustain and grow. Some dots just cannot be disconnected! Here are the 30 dots that **MUST BE CONNECTED!**

1   What are your exit strategies? Are you positioning yourself to be acquired? To be sold? Do you have plans for an IPO?

2   Do you have a multi-scenario business plan?

3   Do you have adequate funding? What are your sources of funding?

4   Have you considered alternate methods of funding?

5   Do you know who will be your primary source of funding at every stage of your business?

6   How is your cash flow managed? Do you have a daily view on your cash situation? Do you have enough money to pay your employees, rent, critical suppliers and bank obligations? Have you stress-tested your cash flow situation? Can you survive in the worst case scenario? If not, do you have contingency plans?

7   Are you over dependent on a single or a few customers? Is this over dependency acceptable risk for your business?

8   Are your key employees emotionally intelligent to deal with the "white water" environment of your small business?

9   Do you know your market and industry structure?

10 What is your incremental value proposition and differentiation relative to your competition?

11 Do you have a purposeful pricing strategy and tactic?

12 Have you designed the end-to- end intentional experience across all touch points that your customers will interact?

13 Do you have branding strategy that all stakeholders of your company can relate to?

14 Do you know how you will engage in a price war if there is one in your industry or market?

15 Are your sales and marketing folks competent to meet your business growth plans?

16 Are your sales teams' compensated to drive wins from your competition?

17 How will you reach the market? Is there an opportunity to create demand through channels other than your sales team?

18 Have you segmented your target customer base? Do you have differentiated propositions and communications for the different segments?

19 Do your marketing communications address the vulnerabilities of human beings? Is it a conscious decision or is it an afterthought?

20 Do you have purposeful strategy to target women? Is it differentiated from your other marketing efforts?

21 Have you considered the end-to-end operations of your business?

22 Do you have policies, procedures and processes that drive productivity in your business?

23 Do you have effective information and telecommunications systems?

24 Do you know where 80% of your cash flow and profits come from?

25 Do you have good, truthful and useful managers?

26 Are you conducting yourself as a leader or are you just a task master?

27 Do you know the set of activities that accentuate your business performance?

28 Do you know the set of activities that diminish your business performance?

29 Do you know how much your business is potentially worth today? Do you know the key variables that drive the value of your business?

30 Is this business really for you?

NOTES

ACKNOWLEDGMENTS

It took me two years of midnight-oil burning to complete *Connect the Dots*, my tribute to the spirit of small and medium business owners. I could never have written this playbook without the encouragement and support of my company, my family, my former bosses and partners and my editorial team. Let's hear the drumroll for:

My bosses, Osman Sultan, CEO of du, Farid Faraidooni, Chief Commercial Officer of du, and Subhra Das, Executive Vice President, Marketing and Customer Experience, du. Osman is one of those rare leaders who have the right component of strategic, operational and people leadership skills. I admire and respect Osman immensely. I thank Farid for showing me what composure and coolness means, even in the most extenuating of circumstances.

I thank Subhra, my immediate boss at du, for helping me to fully understand and internalize that the "proposition is the experience" and that "the experience forms the brand". Unlike many marketers, Subhra is also one of those rare marketing leaders who understand and sow the seeds of growth whilst the company is ahead of its growth curve.

My special gratitude also goes to Hala Badri, EVP Brand and Communications at du, for her steadfast advice and support whilst the book was being written. I deeply appreciate her introductions to key leaders of the UAE business community which helped create a wider awareness about the publication of this book.

My special thanks also go to my former bosses Bill Morrow, Ted Katagi and Gary Cuccio. Three amazing leaders and managers who afforded me the opportunity to work, travel and gain experiences around the world, and showed what leadership is, and how things actually got done.

My thanks also to my former business partners John Thiele and Dinesh Khurana: Great friends and fellow survivors of the "big business flop", who showed me that our friendship meant more than anything else. Even business. Period!

I want to acknowledge my gratitude to my editors Kevin White and Sonali Raha: They waded through an ocean of words and shaped a fun, practical and readable playbook. My special thanks also go to my designer-illustrator Jennifer Swallow. Kevin, Sonali and Jennifer helped me create an informative, reader-friendly content and design that brought the words alive.

Without the involvement of these three individuals, this project would have just remained a pipe dream.

My gratitude also goes out to Ruth Sheehy for the design of the book cover and for the final format and layout of the pages.

I would also like to express my gratitude to Arun Nair, my website designer and search engine optimization (SEO) expert, who taught me how SEO really works.

Anwar Hassan, colleague and friend: Despite having a young family, he tolerated my boring hypothesis and ideas for this book late into many nights.

Jatin Sahni and Vikram Chadha of my team at du; Ryosuke Narikawa, Ryo Akiyama and Marie Austena, from my old team in Vodafone, and many others who reinforced to me and epitomized that people are truly the greatest assets for any company.

My thanks also to the entire team @du who encouraged and gave me moral support for this project: They are fabulous professionals who also gave me valued feedback.

I am deeply indebted to Nadeem Hood and Raquel Almeida for facilitating the logistics and distribution of the book in the Middle East region. I am grateful too to AuthorHouse, the team who turned an idea into paper-and-ink reality.

Last but not least, my sincerest gratitude and appreciation to my darling Carol, who encouraged, motivated, cajoled, nudged and stood by me through thick and thin. Without her love and support, I would never have had the strength to continue and enjoy the career and experiences that I have had. The love of Carol and my children is the very essence of my being. Thank you sweetheart!

And, finally, to every small and medium business owner I have ever met: I admire your spirit and I have learnt from every encounter.

John Lincoln

Author
Dubai and San Francisco
September 2012

HOW TO USE THIS PLAYBOOK

This playbook is meant for YOU. Use it any way you want. But here are a few helpful hints from the author to maximize your experience.

- **Begin at the beginning,** go to the middle and then read through to the end.

- **Or, break the rules.** Begin right at the end for a grand summary and then go back to the beginning for the details.

- **Identify your areas of weakness** and read the chapters that are particularly relevant.

- **Spot your strong points** and double check that you are doing everything right.

- **Jot down your thoughts** and observations at the end of every chapter for a handy, personalized summary.

- **Keep going back to the book** whenever a business question pops into your mind.

- **Have fun reading and learning!** Remember this is a playbook, so don't turn the reading – or your business – into a chore.

- **Ask questions,** comment or just chat with me at johnlincoln@outlook.com

John Lincoln